Fly Fishing the Great Lakes Tributaries

Fly Fishing the Great Lakes Tributaries

Rick Kustich

Illustrated by Jerry Kustich

Frank,
I'd like to take your
guided trip on Bull
Trout Lake. Tight Lines!

Rick Kustich

West River Publishing Company
P.O. Box 15
Grand Island, New York 14072-0015

The Cover: The author releases a 17 pound steelhead caught in a Lake Ontario tributary.
Special thanks to Jay Peck for his assistance in landing and photographing this trophy.

Printed in the United States of America

Library of Congress Catalog Card Number 92-081674

ISBN 0-9633109-0-9

Acknowledgments

The angling fraternity, specifically fly fishers, are for the most part a friendly and helpful group. Although most of this book is based on my personal experiences, a complete coverage of this subject required some assistance from other knowledgeable individuals. I anticipated that such assistance would be easy to find within a group that is so willing to share knowledge. However, the enthusiasm displayed by everyone who played a part in the completion of this work exceeded my expectations.

My brother, Jerry Kustich, who lives in Twin Bridges, Montana, is one of the country's most dedicated fly fishers and has fished across North America. His understanding of the sport combined with his artistic abilities have created instructional illustrations that coordinate with and enhance the text.

My good friend Keith Myott is also an accomplished fly fisher. I commend his patience during many drawn out photography sessions and his willingness to be the subject of many photographs.

I want to extend special thanks to three individuals for their extra effort. To Debra Doerflinger who spent many hours reviewing the original manuscript. Her changes and comments improved the flow of the text and increased its instructional value. To Dave Rust who, with his expertise in the field of photography, had a direct impact on the finished product. He spent time going over equipment and took some of the shots himself, including the color plates of the flies. To Donna Silvestri for her initiative, patience and expertise in the layout and design of the text along with coordinating many aspects of the publishing of this work.

I would also like to express my appreciation to the following friends and acquaintances for their contributions: Jerry Darkes, John Edstrom, John Miller, Mike Modrzynski, Walt Myott, John Sander, Mark Stothard and Les Wedge.

I would also wish to thank the following professional guides who took time from their busy schedules to provide information: Kent Appleby, Pulaski, NY; Troy Creasy, Berwick, PA; Larry Boraas, Algoma, WI; Mike Gnatkowski, Ludington, MI; Jim Rigby, Whitehall, MI; and Fran Verdoliva, Mexico, NY.

My special appreciation goes out to Ann who has supported me through this project since it first began. Her understanding and love of fly fishing has allowed me to spend so much time out on the streams, rivers and lakes.

*To a special place on the
"river" that has forever changed my life.*

Contents

Introduction

In the last decade, the Great Lakes have gained a tremendous reputation for their production of trophy-size fish. In this same period of time, fly fishing has become one of North America's fastest growing forms of recreation. Since almost all of the Great Lakes tributaries can be fly fished, it seems only natural that the two should intersect. Even though fly fishing is becoming popular on Great Lakes tributaries as well, very little has been written dealing directly with this subject. Good fly fishing information does exist on pursuing many of the species of fish found in the Great Lakes. However, no comprehensive guide exists on all the equipment, methods and techniques specifically required to fish the Great Lakes tributaries. The intention of this book is to fill this void.

Even with the popularity of fly fishing, the fly fishing angler is sometimes met with curious looks when fishing the Great Lakes tributaries. Some observe with almost disbelief when fish are hooked and landed by anglers using fly fishing equipment. Many seem to have a preconceived notion that fly fishing is for small fish and another notion that it is a less effective manner of fishing these waters than using the conventional spin fishing gear. However, with the equipment and innovations available to the fly fishing angler today, it seems that a way can be devised to fly fish in almost any type of water and for any kind of fish. In fact, with the efficiency gained through the use of a fly fishing system properly matched with the situation, fly fishing can be more effective than other types of fishing.

The Great Lakes and their tributaries offer a truly great opportunity to take trophy fish on a fly rod. Not everyone has the opportunity to go to Alaska, British Columbia, Labrador or other such places that represent the ultimate in fly fishing for trophy fish. The Great Lakes offer a viable substitute and a great second choice. Admittedly, the esthetics may not be the same as some of these exotic locations, but there are many times when the fishing action on the Great Lakes tributaries is actually better. For that matter, there have been many instances where the esthetics and overall experience have also been top notch. With the vast number of licensed anglers living within a couple hours drive of a Great Lakes tributary, it is obvious that this opportunity exists for many, both residents of Great Lakes states and provinces and their visitors. What is amazing is the amount of serious anglers who are missing out on this opportunity.

The overall lack of available information on this subject has led many Great Lakes anglers to be greatly misinformed. This absence has led to a deterioration of sportsmanlike ethics on some tributaries. The most apparent evidence of this is that some states have allowed the appalling practice of snagging Pacific salmon to be a legal method to take fish. Not only is such a practice in direct contrast with angling values, but has created a barbaric atmosphere on some tributaries and has restricted or even eliminated the opportunities for true sportsman to fish for Pacific salmon on these tributaries. The good news is that snagging seems to be on its last legs in the Great Lakes. Although the laws will probably change much faster than certain people's attitudes will about Pacific salmon, it is a step in the right direction. The abolishment of snagging will undoubtedly be followed by a restoration of fishing ethics and greater opportunity for sport anglers. It takes patience and skill to fair hook Pacific salmon. But considering the fact that each one of these mighty fish is a trophy in itself, it is worth the effort. It's my hope that this book can instill an improved attitude toward Pacific salmon by demonstrating the proper approach, equipment and techniques which will result in consistently fair hooking these fish.

This book is designed as a guide for both novice and seasoned fly fishers. It is basic enough to get the novice started on this type of fishing, yet detailed enough to instruct the experienced fly fisher who is not familiar with the Great Lakes fishery. Hopefully, the experienced angler will find the basic approach of some of this material as a good review of his or her fly fishing knowledge. The book will also be found useful by anglers who have fly fished the tributaries in the past. The overall objective of this book is to design a complete and effective fly fishing system which will allow the angler to enjoy the experience of fishing the Great Lakes tributaries through consistently hooking and landing trophy-size fish.

CHAPTER 1

The Great Lakes

The Great Lakes is the name given to the five freshwater lakes located on the northern border of the lower 48 states. The lakes, comprised of Lake Erie, Lake Huron, Lake Michigan, Lake Ontario and Lake Superior, stretch from the Midwestern part of the United States to the east. This Great Lakes region is one characterized by a wide diversity and is an area upon which Mother Nature has looked favorably. Some of this region, such as the northern shores of Lakes Superior and Huron and Michigan's upper peninsula, have remained unchanged and in some areas uninhabited. On the other end of the spectrum, the shores of the Great Lakes are home to a number of large, densely populated areas including Chicago, Detroit, Cleveland, Toronto, Buffalo and Milwaukee. Despite the attraction for people to settle along their shores, the Great Lakes have remained quite beautiful.

Geographically speaking, the Great Lakes region represents a relatively large area. This is evidenced by approximately 10,000 miles of shoreline located in eight states: Illinois, Indiana, Michigan, Minnesota, New York, Ohio, Pennsylvania and Wisconsin, and one Canadian Province: Ontario. Feeding the lakes throughout the entire region are a vast amount of tributaries–rivers, streams and creeks–providing an almost unlimited opportunity for the fly fisher.

The Great Lakes fishery has seen many changes over the years. During the 1800's, industrialization wiped out a huge Atlantic salmon population in Lake Ontario. In the 1930's through the late 1950's, commercial fishing and the sea lamprey threatened to do the same to the Great Lakes native lake trout population. The sea lamprey was accidently allowed access into the lakes from the ocean. It is a parasite which fastens itself to the outside of its fish host and sucks out the bodily fluids. Adding to the lakes' problems were other species which were also allowed to enter the Great Lakes, namely the alewife and rainbow smelt. They are basically baitfish, which, like the lamprey, came from the ocean and infiltrated the lakes through canals that had been built to link the different Great Lakes' ports for ocean-going ships. With a lack of predation caused by the lamprey's destruction of native populations, the numbers of alewife and smelt in the lakes soared. Incredible amounts of these fish died each year and were washed ashore, creating an unbearable stench.

Not only was the lake trout fishery in trouble, but native warm water species were suffering as well. Much of this stemmed from a significant decline in water quality. The Great Lakes became a dumping ground for various types of industrial and agricultural waste. Such pollutants dramatically changed the make up of the lakes.

Something had to change or this fishery might very well be lost forever. By the late 1950's some hope became evident. A selective toxicant called TFM was found. This substance, added to breeding areas, would kill lampreys without doing much damage to other species. The lamprey problem came under control. Also around this time, water quality began to improve. This was precipitated by an awareness that the lakes were steadily being poisoned and that new controls had to be put into effect.

Even with these improvements in the Great Lakes environment, the population of predators, such as the lake trout, did not bounce back as rapidly as anticipated. The result of this was a continued overabundance of baitfish. Something else was needed. In 1966 and throughout the rest of the 1960's, a program was begun which would change the complexion of the Great Lakes. Coho and chinook salmon, transplanted from the Pacific ocean, were introduced into Lake Michigan and Lake Superior in 1966 and into the other three lakes in 1968. The program was met with almost immediate success. Not only did the salmon control populations of alewives and smelt, but created, almost instantly, a quality fishery for trophy-size salmon. The fishery was maintained through stockings.

On the coattails of the introduction of the Pacific salmon were other planting programs. In the 1970's, rainbow and brown trout were stocked throughout the Great Lakes. Lake trout stocking was stepped up and brook trout were planted in some areas. These stocking programs were also successful and the fish were big. Even though some of the lakes were already host to some of these species before such programs, their populations were now at a level to provide a great opportunity to catch trophy trout and char in addition to trophy salmon.

The success story continued through the 1980's. The introduced species grew even bigger, and with continued improvement in water quality and some stocking programs, native warm water species enjoyed a steady comeback as well. As anglers learned more about the fish and their habits, the fishing experience continued to get better. Although the Great Lakes fishery as we know it today is just passing the point of its infancy, it is already, in all probability, the best fresh water fishery in the world.

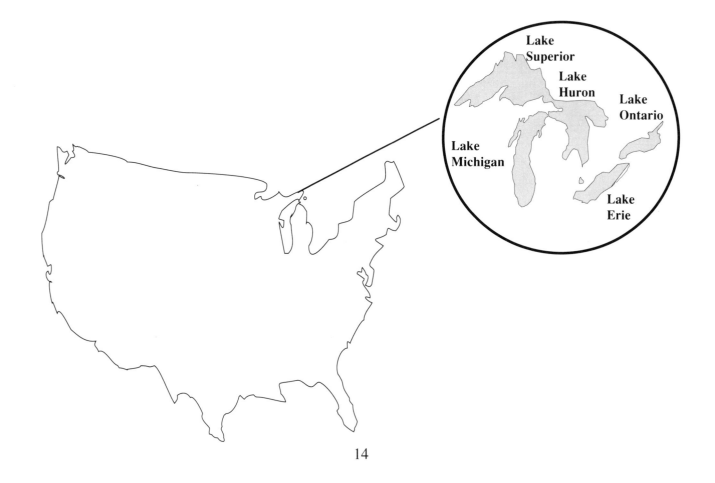

CHAPTER 2

Trophy Fish of the Great Lakes

Most tributaries to the Great Lakes are host to a wide variety of fish. While some make these tributaries their year-round home, many spend most of their lives within the Great Lakes and utilize the tributaries for spawning or occasionally to take advantage of a feeding opportunity. The main focus of this book is the latter group. Those fish which live in the forage-rich lakes grow to trophy proportions and become susceptible to the fly fishing angler as they enter the tributaries, or in the areas of the lake near the tributaries. Most of the fish in this group are comprised of the salmonid family. This family includes all salmon, trout and char. Salmonids reach the greatest size of the common Great Lakes species and consequently put up the heart-pounding type of fight that tests the angler's skill and equipment. In addition, salmonids are distributed throughout the entire Great Lakes region.

Since salmon, trout and char, as well as warm water species, all have a specific purpose for being in or near the tributaries, it is imperative that the angler have an understanding of the characteristics of each species. This understanding will help determine the time of year to be on the stream, the equipment, the type of water to fish, the method to use and even the fly to tie on to the end of the leader. Since this understanding is so important, it is a logical beginning point.

PACIFIC SALMON

There are three species of salmon native to the Pacific Ocean which now inhabit the Great Lakes. They are the chinook, coho and pink salmon. The chinooks are widely distributed throughout the Great Lakes and are the most abundant of all salmonids. Cohos have a moderate distribution throughout all the lakes while the pink salmon are mainly confined to Lake Superior, Lake Huron and a moderate population in Lake Erie. The chinook or king not only boasts the greatest numbers but also is the largest of the Great Lakes salmonids. Fish from 15 to 30 pounds are common. In Lake Ontario, chinooks near or exceeding 40 pounds are taken each year. It is important to note, however, that the average size of a chinook or any other species will vary from lake to lake depending on such factors as the forage base, the growing season, and general habitat.

Chinooks begin to filter into the tributaries in August and even earlier in some Michigan and other Midwestern rivers. The peak of the run usually occurs from mid-September to mid-October on most tributaries. As they move into the streams they begin to take on their spawning colors, changing from silver in the lake to a greenish hue and then to a darker almost black appearance. When the chinook was first introduced, it was quickly pegged as a fish that did not feed once it entered a tributary to spawn. It seemed as though its reputation preceded it from the West Coast where it is a biological fact that the feeding mechanism of these mighty fish shuts down as they enter the tributary to spawn and energy is used to satisfy the spawning urge. This phenomenon is also true

A chinook salmon.

for Great Lakes kings. However, it is also a well proven fact that, although not actively feeding, they will strike! The trick here is to play on their aggressive behavior while on or near their spawning beds. Others suggest that the strike might be an impulsive response to a food source. Putting theory aside, the important thing is that the opportunity exists to tie into these bruisers on the fly rod.

The fact that chinooks readily strike while in the tributaries is something that many people cannot, or simply will not, accept as truth. It has been proven time and time again that they do take flies. Additionally, due to the control it provides, fly fishing seems to be the best approach for chinooks in the tributaries.

Chinooks on their spawning beds seem to represent the best opportunity for the fly fisher. Even though some anglers prefer fishing holding areas for chinooks as they make their way up the tributary, more hookups will be experienced while fishing to spawning fish. Their behavior sometimes becomes so aggressive while on or near their spawning beds that they will chase, nip or bite anything that comes near them. This can be another salmon's tail, other species of fish attempting to prey on eggs or the angler's fly.

The males, which can be distinguished from the female by their darker appearance, are normally more aggressive than the females. The optimal situation seems to be when fresh fish move into an active bedding area. This situation is intensified further when the males greatly outnumber the available females. This brings a particular day to mind. Both males and females were so aggressive that almost every fly that passed their way was either chased or taken. Normally one male will be the dominant fish. It will not always be the biggest but it will be the most aggressive. The angler should target this fish.

The coho has similar habits as the chinook when it comes to its spawning run. It also takes on its spawning colors as it enters the river and usually can be distinguished from the chinook by a reddish hue on its side. However, they tend to begin their run slightly later than the king. To the favor of the angler, the coho is usually more aggressive in the stream, many times moving right off its bed to chase and take an intruding fly. Coho are smaller in size than a chinook with the average fish in the fall weighing 5 to 10 pounds, and are also smaller in numbers. The lower numbers are mainly the result of past and present stocking practices. Fewer cohos have been planted apparently since they are smaller than the king and because the summer angling success for this species in the lake is inconsistent. Additionally, even though they are more easily caught once in the tributary than a chinook, many times a coho will only spend a few days in the tributary's main body and then shoot up to its headwaters or dam leaving little angling opportunity throughout the tributary.

A bonus fly fishing opportunity exists for the angler in the early spring right after ice-out for both chinook and coho. In western Lake Ontario, this happens in April and exists through May. At this time of year, the fly fishing for the salmon takes place right in the lake itself. The fish are in close to shore, usually near the mouths of the streams and rivers, taking advantage of the warmer water temperatures and feeding voraciously on baitfish. The fish are now bright silver and are full of spunk when hooked. The opportunity exists for the angler to wade into the lake itself near these

mouths and cast baitfish patterns to fool the feeding salmon. Another productive approach is to work the shallows near the mouth utilizing a boat or a float tube. Both can produce heart-stopping hits and hookups. In the spring the average size of the chinook and coho is considerably less than in the fall after a summer full of feeding, but the fight of a bright chinook in the lake is unparalleled. Also, in the spring the chinook and coho are similar in appearance. The best way to tell the two apart is that the chinooks have a black pigment at the base of their carnivorous teeth while cohos have white at the base of their teeth. This can also be used for identification in the fall.

The pink salmon, or "humpie" as they are referred to because of the hump that develops on their backs during their spawning run, are not widely distributed throughout the Great Lakes. Pinks are generally not a large fish. They average 1 to 4 pounds, but the streams that get consistent runs can produce some fine angling. In the streams where natural reproduction does occur, the runs have been getting stronger. Like the chinook and coho, the pink runs in the fall.

Since all the Pacific salmon species inhabiting the Great Lakes die after spawning, fish caught earlier in the run are healthier and put up a better fight. Fish caught late into the run are beginning to deteriorate and can be disappointing fighters. Another thing to remember is that these salmon will, in general, return to the stream where they were hatched or planted. Some tributaries do not have sufficient water quality to support natural reproduction of Pacific salmon or other salmon species and are supported solely by stocking programs. Even in the tributaries that do not support reproduction, fish that return will go through all the phases of spawning. By finding out information on what streams have good reproduction or which ones have had heavy stockings in prior years, the angler can anticipate good runs in future years.

In general, mature chinooks and cohos return to spawn after three years, although some return as early as 1 year and as late as 5. One factor which will obviously determine the size of the fish upon return to the stream will be the amount of years it spent in the lake. The pink salmon generally return after 2 years.

STEELHEAD/RAINBOW

The New York State Department of Conservation and the American Fisheries Society consider the steelhead and rainbow to be the same species of fish. The steelhead is distinguished from domestic rainbow in that the former is a migratory strain and the latter is a non-migratory strain of rainbow trout. In theory, migratory fish will imprint on one stream where they were hatched or stocked and return to it to spawn, while non-migratory fish will not necessarily return to the same stream. Since any differences between them are not significant, all lake-run rainbows will be referred to as steelhead.

The chinook may be known as a "king" but the steelhead is the reigning king of the Great Lakes. Its strong and acrobatic style of fighting

A steelhead caught during the spring spawning run.

makes it the most exciting fish inhabiting the tributaries. This fish already has a rich history in the Great Lakes. Steelhead were first introduced into this region in the late 1800's. This original introduction resulted in natural reproduction in some tributaries. The steelhead program in the Great Lakes was then stepped up in the early 1970's along with the other salmonids.

Steelhead generally average 6 to 12 pounds throughout its Great Lakes range with fish in excess of 20 pounds caught occasionally. To land one of these torpedoes in the 15 to 20 pound range on fly tackle takes all the angler's skill, not to mention a little luck. Though the exhilarating fight generates much of the angler enthusiasm, there are other reasons that make the steelhead the most popular of the lake-run salmonids. They are widely distributed, and virtually every Great Lakes tributary receives some sort of steelhead run which creates fishing opportunities for those who prefer to avoid the more popular streams. Even streams that have never been planted with steelhead receive runs of fish which have not imprinted on a particular stream. Thanks to these straying fish, streams and rivers with high water quality and good spawning conditions common in Michigan, Ontario and Wisconsin now support good, consistent runs based entirely on natural reproduction.

The opportunity for the fly fisher to tie into a trophy steelhead is further increased by the amount of time the steelhead remains in the tributaries. Certain strains of fall steelhead begin to enter the tributaries as early as September with the peak of the fall run occurring in late October through December. Although the steelhead do not spawn until early spring, they will winter in the tributary. Steelhead will continue to filter into the tributaries during January and early February if water conditions permit. The run begins to intensify again in late February in some streams, and peaks in March and April. Some fish remain until May or June. The fall and winter fishing is in pools, pockets and other holding water. The spring fishing is usually confined to the gravelly runs where the steelies congregate to spawn.

As an added bonus, a number of states have introduced Skamania strain steelhead to their streams. These fish are summer run steelhead entering the streams as early as June. They continue to run through July and August, creating a year round fishery in some areas. Unfortunately, these summer run fish seem to only run in streams in the summer months which have optimum water temperature and quality. Currently, several Michigan streams and rivers and a few in Indiana are experiencing decent runs of summer fish.

Unlike the chinook and coho, the steelhead continues to feed once it enters the tributary. Although they are sometimes finicky and difficult to get to take, there are times when steelhead have gone on the feed to the point of a frenzy, with nearly every angler on the river getting in on the action. Normally, their feeding activity falls somewhere between the two extremes. There are times when the fly fishing angler will be fishing to feeding steelhead and times when he or she will be fishing to spawning steelhead. The distinction is important because it will dictate the equipment, fly and technique to be used. To complicate matters, there are times when spawning steelhead will take time out from their activities to feed.

Steelhead are also susceptible to fly fishing in the lake both in the fall and early spring as they congregate at the river mouths to begin their upstream migration as well as late spring after the run, either in the shallows or near the top in deeper water. A few steelhead can even be found all winter in the lake near the river mouths. These fish seem to prefer the current flow as it enters the lake, possibly because it acts as a constant food source. Also, look for fish in the winter and early spring near and around warm water discharges created by the many power generation stations located along the shores of the Great Lakes.

19

A heavy lake-run brown trout.

BROWN TROUT

From the inhabitants of the small inland trout streams to the behemoths of the Great Lakes, there is a mystique that is unique to the brown trout. Given its somewhat reclusive nature, it is certainly one of the most intriguing of all game fish. It is this opportunity to fly fish for huge browns in the Great Lakes that makes reality exceed the dreams of many fly fishing anglers.

Although not as exciting a fighter as the steelhead, the brown does put up a strong battle that sometimes tires the angler before the fish is tired. Dressed in their fall spawning colors and males with their hooked jaws, lake-run brown trout are a pretty fish. The browns normally begin their spawning run in late September and continue to enter the streams through October and November, the peak being the end of October or beginning of November. Some of these fish will linger into the winter months and will make up a portion of the winter steelheader's catch.

When the brown trout enters the tributary, it will usually feed freely and take a wide range of flies from egg patterns to nymphs to streamers. Then as the brown becomes more interested in spawning in November, it beds up and usually becomes a little more difficult to entice into striking. Finally, as the spawning ritual draws to an end, the brown enters a feeding period before dropping back to the lake.

Though the brown trout can be found in all

of the Great Lakes, the largest concentrations exist in Lake Ontario and Lake Michigan due in large part to past planting practices. It is interesting to note that not all tributaries receive consistent runs of browns. It is important to determine which tributaries do get runs before setting out for this species. The average size of a Great Lakes brown trout is in the 5 to 10 pound range, with fish up to and exceeding 20 pounds occasionally caught in the tributaries. Even larger browns up to and exceeding 30 pounds have been taken. The opportunity exists to fly fish for monsters of this size in the spring when they, too, move into the lake shallows to feed as do the salmon and steelhead.

Many times brown trout are caught while the angler is pursuing salmon and steelhead, and basically make up a bonus catch in those tributaries which only receive sporadic runs. However, there are occasions when a tributary will be so loaded with browns that even fast-paced fly fishing for trophy class fish is possible. In addition to spring lake fishing for browns, a few rivers receive a spring run of fish in their lower ends. A heavy concentration of baitfish usually prompts this situation, and such a condition can produce excellent fly fishing. The lower ends of tributaries and their mouths are also a good place to explore in September with baitfish patterns as the browns begin their run. Many opportunities exist to tangle with the Great Lakes brown on the fly rod.

LAKE TROUT

From a management standpoint, a different emphasis has been placed on the "laker" over the years. The species discussed to this point have all been planted and sustained with the intention of controlling the forage fish base and providing a recreational fishery. Since the lake trout is native to the Great Lakes, the management approach has been that of a restoration project. The success of this project seems to be somewhat limited. However, it is a long-term strategy with greater success

envisioned for the future. Currently, the population of lake trout throughout the Great Lakes is largely supported by annual plantings and is widely distributed throughout the Great Lakes.

Few think of the lake trout as a fish to be pursued with a fly rod. Others who have only come in contact with lake trout while trolling and utilizing downriggers may not be overly impressed with their fight. However, put one of these vicious hitters at the end of a fly rod and the fish takes on an entirely different character. A successful battle with a big lake trout usually leaves the fly fishing angler with a smile and an aching forearm from its strong fighting style.

Great Lakes lake trout average around 5 to 10 pounds, with fish from 10 to 16 pounds caught on a regular basis. The fly fishing opportunities that exist for lake trout are wide and varied throughout the Great Lakes. Some streams and rivers actually receive runs of fish. Lakers run into these tributaries mainly for feeding purposes. Some streams and rivers receive both fall and spring runs. Many times these runs are limited to the lower ends of the tributary. Due to the varied intensities of runs, it is important to learn rivers in the areas in which you intend to fish. It is a must to find these consistent lake trout runs in order to cash in on this fishing. New York's Niagara River receives a strong run in the spring and fall where other tributaries nearby receive none. Baitfish patterns and egg patterns are consistent producers on these river-running lakers.

The most wide-spread lake trout opportunity for the fly fisher exists in the early spring in the lakes. Lakers will be found near the mouths of tributaries and cruising close to shore, just waiting to smash baitfish patterns. The fly caster can get to the lake trout by wading or using a float tube. Probably the best bet is to use a small, open aluminum boat. Lakers fight very well in this cold water, and such fishing really needs to be experienced to be appreciated.

The lake trout has a very slow growth rate

A beautiful lake trout photographed before its release.

when compared to other Great Lakes trout and salmon. Given this fact, and the overall management strategy as previously discussed, special regulations exist in certain areas. Be familiar with such regulations and be sure to release any out-of-season fish carefully. For that matter, the lake trout is a good fish to release under any condition.

BROOK TROUT

When one thinks of the Great Lakes fishing opportunities, brook trout are usually one species that does not come to mind, but the opportunity does exist for trophy brookies. Although native to the Great Lakes, they are not widely distributed. Decent populations can be found in the northern part of Lake Michigan, Lake Huron and throughout Lake Superior. Most of the brook trout, or coasters as they are referred to, show up in the streams or shorelines of Michigan, Minnesota, Ontario and Wisconsin. Though there is some natural reproduction, Wisconsin seems to have the best concentration resulting from planting the most fish over the years.

Lake-run brook trout do not grow to the size of other Great Lakes species. They average around 3 pounds, with some growing to 5 pounds or larger. The Nipigon River, a tributary located on the north shore of Lake Superior, lays claim to the world record brook trout. It weighed 14 pounds and 8 ounces and was caught in 1916.

The coasters remain in fairly shallow water all year round, and although they can be caught in the spring, the best opportunity exists in late August and September. At this time the brook trout begin to congregate off the river mouths to begin their fall run. Fishing these areas by wading or using a boat can be as productive as fishing the tributaries. Streamers work best in the lake. Natural patterns such as various nymphs are preferred in the tributaries.

Since the coasters do not run into every tributary, it is important to become familiar with the specific streams or areas that have brook trout runs in order to enjoy fly fishing success on this species.

ATLANTIC SALMON

Recent attempts have been made to plant Atlantic salmon in the Great Lakes by the states of Michigan and New York and the Province of Ontario. The stocking of this species in Lake Ontario by New York and Ontario essentially represents an attempt to restore Atlantic salmon to its native habitat.

At this point in time, the Atlantic salmon plantings have been met with only limited success. Since Great Lakes Atlantics enter the tributaries in the summer or early fall when the weather is pleasant and take a fly willingly, they would provide excellent sport at an otherwise slow time of year for tributary fishing. There is good news. New York has announced that it is stepping up its Atlantic salmon stocking program. Actually, the Black River, at the eastern end of Lake Ontario, will no longer be stocked with chinooks. The emphasis will be put on the Atlantic salmon. Atlantics were planted in this scenic river during 1990, and Ontario has also stepped up its program. One can only hope that this fishery realizes its potential.

WARM WATER SPECIES

Salmonids are not the only trophy fish available to the fly fishing angler in the Great Lakes. The tributaries host some excellent fly fishing for a variety of warm water species which can also grow to trophy proportions. Smallmouth and largemouth bass, walleye, muskellunge and northern pike can all be taken on the fly rod utilizing the same basic methods used to fool salmonids. As a matter of fact, many of these warm water species are caught while in pursuit of trophy salmon, trout and char.

Some of these fish reside in the tributary year-round while others spend some or most of their time in the lake and move into the streams and rivers to spawn or feed. Often these species can be found near the mouths of these tributaries throughout the summer. Some of the streams or rivers will be host to all of these warm water species and others may hold just one or even none. Again, it is important to find which tributaries hold which fish before you plan your attack.

Walleye, muskellunge and northern are all suckers for big baitfish patterns. Smallmouths react well to natural patterns which represent such food sources as crayfish, nymphs and leeches, as well as baitfish patterns. While largemouths also love leech and baitfish patterns, frog imitations and

Smallmouth bass are one of the warm water species which can be pursued in the Great Lakes with the fly rod.

other deer hair bass flies work well.

These species can usually be found in the tributaries from early spring through fall and can sometimes provide action when there are no trout and salmon to be found in the streams or rivers, particularly in the summer. These species all spawn in the spring which can be a great time for hot and heavy action. One should check local regulations before pursuing spawning warm water species, for in some states such fish are protected when on their spawning beds.

CHAPTER 3

Equipment

As noted in the introduction, there seems to be a preconceived notion among many anglers that all fly fishing equipment is designed for fishing for trout on small streams, and therefore all fly rods are long and wispy to provide a sporting fight for such small stream fish. Actually, this is a myth.

Although the first fly rods were in fact soft, produced of split bamboo and designed for poetic casting to rising trout on fertile streams, time has a way of changing everything. In the fly fishing world, this could not be more apparent. Today rods and reels are engineered to hook and land big fish, from salmon on the Pacific coast in the 40 to 60 pound range to tarpon in the 100 to 200 pound range! Indeed, equipment is an important part of developing a system to consistently enjoy success on the Great Lakes tributaries. However, purchasing the best equipment money can buy is not necessarily the answer. It is more important to match the fly tackle, regardless of quality and price, to the quarry for which it is intended.

RODS

Since the early days of fly fishing and the use of split bamboo rods, other materials have impacted rod construction. Today nearly all the rods built that are suitable for this type of fly fishing are made of either fiberglass, graphite or boron. Each has its advantages and disadvantages when compared to one another. The important factor is to match the rod size and material with the desired fly fishing situation. Unlike a spinning rod which is designed for a certain range of lure weights, a fly rod is engineered for a specific fly line weight. Lines carry weight designations of 1 through 15 with each number representing a certain weight of the first 30 feet of that line. The greater the number, the heavier the line. Each rod is specifically designed for a certain weight line which is usually stated on the butt section of the rod. Heavier line weights cast longer and are matched with stronger rods designed to handle the heavier weight of the line. Lighter line weights, in general, are used for more delicate casting situations and are matched with lighter rods. The line weight designation is a standard, and a line with a certain weight designation, an 8 weight line for example, will essentially weigh the same among all different manufacturers.

In many fly fishing situations, the type and size of line required usually dictates the rod to be used. However, in most situations in the Great Lakes tributary fishery, the rod selection is made by the requirement of the fighting strength of the rod. In other words, first the rod is chosen that will physically handle these trophies, and then the proper line is used to balance the system. On the other hand, there are also some situations where a rod is chosen which handles a heavy enough line weight required to cast long distances or throw big flies. Often this is necessary on big rivers or in the lakes.

In general, a rod built for a 9 to 11 weight line will handle the stress and strain of a Great

Chart of Line Weight Ranges

Line Weight Designation #	Weight-Grains* First 30 Feet of Line	Tolerance
1	60	Plus or Minus 6 Grains
2	80	Plus or Minus 6 Grains
3	100	Plus or Minus 6 Grains
4	120	Plus or Minus 6 Grains
5	140	Plus or Minus 6 Grains
6	160	Plus or Minus 8 Grains
7	185	Plus or Minus 8 Grains
8	210	Plus or Minus 8 Grains
9	240	Plus or Minus 10 Grains
10	280	Plus or Minus 10 Grains
11	330	Plus or Minus 12 Grains
12	380	Plus or Minus 12 Grains

*(437-1/2 Grains=1 ounce)

Lakes salmon, while a 7 to 9 weight rod will normally be sufficient for handling steelhead and other Great Lakes trout and char. Logic may dictate here that the stronger the rod the better for battling these big fish. However, the stronger rods handling heavy lines are usually physically heavier which makes them more tiring to cast during a day's outing. Therefore, a happy medium must be reached during the choice of a rod. It must be light enough to cast comfortably and strong enough to handle the size of fish inhabiting the Great Lakes.

This brings the discussion back to the various fly rod materials available. Fiberglass is the least expensive of the materials. In some cases, due to its thickness in the butt section, it is the strongest for fighting purposes. During one particular fall of salmon fishing, one fishing partner consistently hooked and landed big chinooks on an 11 weight glass rod which he dubbed the "Salmon Slayer" due to its great fighting strength. It was one of the only rods which actually tired out the salmon before the angler in heavy water situations. However, fiberglass rods tend to be heavier than boron or graphite rods built for the same line weights.

The lighter boron and graphite rods offer greater sensitivity, strength and a faster casting action. A faster casting action means that the power of the rod is located near the middle of the rod extending through the tip; a slower action is centered more through the butt section. Boron rods tend to be thinner than graphite without sacrificing strength. Boron also tends to be more expensive than graphite, a feature that makes graphite the popular choice of Great Lakes fly fishing anglers. The introduction of new higher modulus graphite has resulted in rods that are lighter and stronger yet.

Rod length is another important consideration. Here the choice seems to be more simple.

Longer rods of 9 to 10 feet seem to work best. The longer rod allows the angler to get his or her line off or out of the water more easily and is better for longer casts which are required in big pools and on the open water of the lake. Also, longer rods are an advantage in tight casting situations where roll casts and other innovative casting strokes are needed.

My choice for a steelhead and trout rod is a strong 9-1/2 foot for an 8 weight graphite with a medium to fast casting action. Its strength allows for a firm hook set and the medium to fast action lends to good line control when casting or mending. A characteristic of a strong rod is that it can easily handle a line weight of even two weight designations higher than for which it is actually built. The heavier line weight can make both close and distant casting easier. Moving up line weights is a characteristic of a good graphite rod and is a common trait of boron due to the general strength of that material. Whether a rod can handle higher line weights can be determined simply by casting other lines and seeing whether the outfit remains in balance.

As for a salmon rod, the preference is for a 9-1/2 foot for a 10 weight graphite possessing similar qualities to the steelhead and trout rod desired above. A 10 foot for an 11 weight graphite rod is a good choice in some situations. These are mainly in heavy water where extra strength is needed or when fishing for salmon from a boat when only a limited number of casts is required and the extra weight of the rod is not a problem.

Anyone who is serious about pursuing salmonids year round in the Great Lakes tributaries should have one outfit for trout and char and one for chinooks. This does not necessarily require a major cash outlay since there are a number of reasonably priced quality rods on the market today. As a matter of fact, with the number of rods on the market, choosing one can be quite a task. By keeping the important features in mind, talking to knowledgeable anglers and by actually casting the

rod, the proper selection can be made. Additionally, the rod should feel comfortable in the angler's hand when gripped. There are a number of different grips, and each angler has a preference. If the rod chosen does not have the preferred grip, it most likely can be custom ordered. Also, a rod with an extended fighting butt can be a real advantage especially for the arm that tires from fights provided by chinooks and big steelhead.

As mentioned, there are a number of rods on the market of various quality and price. The following are just some of the manufacturers producing rods of sufficient quality: Cortland, Fenwick, G. Loomis, J. Kennedy-Fisher, Orvis, R.L. Winston, Sage, St. Croix and Scott Power Ply.

REELS

Many anglers are led to believe that the fly reel's main purpose is for storing line and that the clicking noise of a single action reel is simply the mechanism which prevents backlashing. When the angler's only fly fishing pursuit is small stream bred trout, such a belief is basically true and this understanding is sufficient.

However, when in pursuit of big game fish, the reel becomes a integral part of one's equipment. The reel must be built to withstand the rigors of fishing for big fish, and a greater understanding of the general mechanics of such reels is important to assure that the one chosen is a good match for its intended use.

One of the first considerations of a Great Lakes fly reel is its physical size. It must be big enough to handle the larger diameter 7 to 11 weight lines along with 100 to 200 yards of backing. In addition, it must be durable to withstand the wild runs of fresh lake-run fish. Its design and construction must provide quality service. A good sign of quality design and construction is a smooth spinning spool with little or no wobble.

The drag system in a Great Lakes fly reel is a very important aspect of this piece of equipment. The drag system is what creates resistance as line is run out of the reel. In addition to preventing backlashes, its purpose is to tire the fish along with slowing or stopping its run. There are basically two types of drag systems to consider. First is the click drag which is created by a spring and pawl design in the reel. This click drag is sometimes combined with a palming feature created by an exposed outer spool. By using the palm of the hand, the angler can add extra resistance to the spool to slow or stop the run of a fish. The second basic design is a disk or shoe type drag which actually works in a similar manner to brakes on an automobile, with two hard surfaces being pressed against each other to create resistance. Drag systems should be adjustable to control the amount of resistance. However, since there is more to a disk drag, a reel with this system will normally be heavier than one with a click type.

Another aspect of a fly reel important to its performance is the manner in which the line comes off the spool. With a direct drive reel, a turn of the handle results in a turn of the spool, with the spool and handle rotating quickly when a fish runs out line. Conversely, the spool anti-reverse reel prevents the handle from turning as line is run off the spool.

Finally, the action of the reel should be

This demonstrates the difference between a click type drag on the left and a disk type drag on the right.

considered. There are two types, the single action and the multiplier. With a single action reel, one rotation of the handle results in one rotation of the spool. Conversely, one full rotation of the handle of a multiplying reel results in more than one rotation of the spool. The result is that the multiplier picks up line faster than a single action reel. This is a real advantage when a hot fish decides to make a run right at the angler. This feature is not necessary, and a single action reel will work fine in most situations.

For trout, char and most warm water species, a single action reel will work well in most situations. Either a click type or disk drag will suffice. My preference is for the lighter weight click drag since it can be fished more comfortably for a longer period of time. It is recommended that a reel that has a click drag also have an exposed outer spool so that the angler can manually add drag when the situation arises. Additional drag can also be added by allowing the line to run through the index finger and middle finger of the rod hand. This can be a good technique to use with a reel that does not have an exposed outer spool. A good approach is to keep the drag set light and add tension manually as necessary. This seems to help land more fish and minimize breakoffs when using light tippets.

When it comes to fishing for chinooks the preference is for a heavy-duty reel. A spool anti-reverse reel can prevent bloody knuckles, especially when fishing heavy, fast water which can intensify the fish's speed as it runs out line. A disk drag system is normally the best choice when fishing for salmon. The tippets used for salmon are generally heavy and strong. The disk drag combined with strong tippets allows the angler to tighten the tension to the point where it makes it difficult for the fish to take out line. This allows the angler to tire the fish more quickly and control the fight. A good disk drag system also generally has the capacity to handle lighter tippets.

The proper choice of one reel with a few

extra spools can serve both as a reel for trout as well as for salmon. When the angler switches rods to one requiring a different weight line, he or she can simply change spools with a matching line. However, there may be times when an angler may prefer having a couple reels with different features for varying fishing conditions as previously discussed. As with fly rods, there are a vast number of reels available that will get the job done. The cost of these reels varies even more than rods, but good quality can be found at all price ranges. The following is a list of some of the companies which produce quality and dependable reels suitable for Great Lakes fly fishing: Abel Reels, ATH Design (Ari T Hart), Browning, Cortland, G. Loomis, Hardy USA, Inc., Lamson USA, Martin Reel Co., Orvis, Peerless, Regal Engineering Inc., Ross Reels, Scientific Anglers, Shakespeare (Medalist Reels), STH Reels, Stream Line, Thomas and Thomas, Tycoon-Finoor and Val-Craft, Inc. (Valentine Reels).

Various reels and spools used in Great Lakes fly fishing.

LINES

The discussion of lines began in the section dealing with rods. The topic of line weight was examined relative to rod design. Also discussed was the concept of the line weight designation number and that it is a standard based on a line's actual weight. Nevertheless, a variety of lines exists within each weight designation, each possessing different qualities and each serving a specific purpose to meet the needs of the fly fishing angler. The type of line used for fishing the Great Lakes and its tributaries will mainly be determined by the technique being used or the water being fished.

The most common and possibly most popular among Great Lakes fly anglers is the full-floating line. This line is designed to float on the surface and if properly cared for will maintain this property throughout its life. Although the floating line may be more commonly associated with dry fly fishing for trout, it is an invaluable tool for presenting the fly in a natural drag free manner. Even though there are some opportunities to take Great Lakes species at or near the surface, most fish are caught on or near the bottom. This requires that the angler get the fly down to the fish. For this reason, when using a floating line, the fly will usually need to be weighted or lead will need to be added to the leader. Casting lead is not considered the most pleasant of fly casting methods, but the floating line allows the angler to have the most control of his or her fly. The length of the leader must vary with the change in water depth. This will be discussed further in this chapter.

In contrast to the full-floater, the basic idea with the full-sinking line is that the sinking property combined with a short leader will take the fly down to the fish. These lines come in a wide variety of sink rates from slow (a sink rate of approximately 1.25 inches per second) to very fast (a sink rate of 6.5 inches per second). The depth and type of water will determine which is required.

The sink-tip line is essentially a combination of the first two line types discussed. It is basically a fusion of a part of a sinking line with a part of a floating line. The tip portion, as the name implies, consists of a sinking line with the remaining portion possessing a floating quality. The concept of the sink-tip is to take advantage of the sinking line's ability to get the fly down and the floating line's capacity for line control. A wide variety of sink-tip lines exists on the market which vary in the length of the sinking section and can be found in all the sink rates available for full-sinking lines. Sink-tips with a sinking section of 10 to 13 feet seem to be the most versatile and best accomplish the potential of the sink-tip's design. The angler should not be confused or overwhelmed by the wide selection of sink-tips and should not feel that it is necessary to own one of each. Usually one or two can be chosen which are best suited for the water which the angler frequents.

It is important that an understanding is gained of the capabilities of each sink-tip and that it is properly matched with the fishing conditions. In addition to commercially manufactured sink-tips, one can custom produce his or her own by splicing a section of a sinking line with a section of a floater. This may be necessary for some special situations and was popular for innovative fly fishers of years gone by. With the lines on the market today, there is a manufactured sink-tip for almost every situation.

Another type of line which can be an important part of the Great Lakes fly fishing angler's arsenal is the shooting head. The shooting head gets its name from its length and not from the basic characteristics as in the other line types. It is a short fly line, generally only 25 to 35 feet. Some are even quite shorter. It generally has the same weight as the first 30 feet of a full line of the same weight designation. In other words, the first 30 feet of an 8 weight sinking line weighs the same as an 8 weight shooting head, but the shooting head may have this weight concentrated in a much

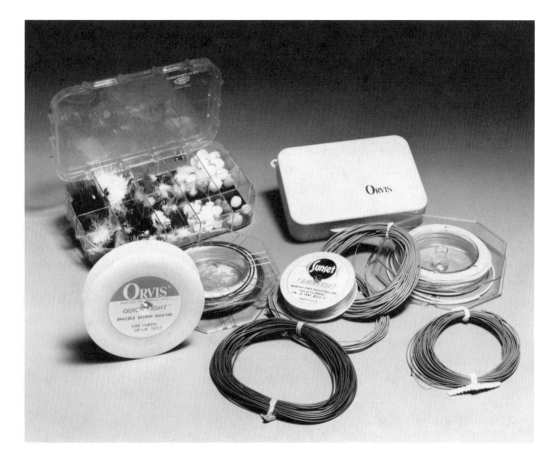

Various lines and coiled shooting heads used in fly fishing the Great Lakes and their tributaries.

shorter area. This feature combined with a low diameter shooting line allows the angler to cast this type of line a long way. The ability to make long casts is of particular importance when fly fishing the lake or big pools of large rivers.

Shooting heads can be either floating or sinking with a variety of sink rates. The ability to fish great depths can be the key feature of the shooting head. There are some heads available that will get deeper than any other fly line. These are the Deep Water Express lines produced by Scientific Anglers and Kerboom produced by Cortland. They have a sink rate of between 7 to 10-3/4 inches per second and a weight range of between 450 and 850 grains (note that the weight of the first thirty feet of a 9 weight line is 240 grains). Most of the time these lines are cut down

so that they are easier to handle. The Deep Water Express is available in the heaviest weight, 850 grains. Kerboom seems to have a slightly greater sink rate. Due to their sink rate, these lines hold a place in Great Lakes fly fishing.

Along with the various commercially produced shooting heads, homemade shooting heads can be created from a level plastic coated lead core line manufactured by Cortland called LC-13. This material weighs 13 grains per foot, so a line of 18 feet balances a 9 weight rod. However, my preference is a range of line lengths from 10 to 25 feet with the longer, heavier lines being capable of reaching greater depths than the shorter ones. With this variety, a number of different depths can be covered. Another value of creating your own heads is that it is an inexpensive way to put together a collection of fast sinking lines. The inexpensive feature is also a plus when fishing deep in areas that are filled with snags and where the possibility exists that an entire shooting head can be lost. It does happen, but it is a lot easier to take when the head only costs a couple bucks. Homemade shooting heads are created by forming a loop at one end of the line.

There are a number of techniques used to create this loop. The easiest entails simply doubling back a small section of line, approximately 3/4 of an inch, to form the loop. The loop is secured with heavy fly tying thread using a bobbin and a fly tying vice. The heavy thread is important since strong wraps are required to dig into the coating of the line. The wraps are completed with a whip finish. The end of the line should be cut on an angle so that when the wraps are complete, there is a tapered effect to the loop. Epoxy can be added to the wraps to strengthen the loop. Aquaseal should be added to create a smooth coating to enable the loop to more easily slide through the guides. The one disadvantage of this loop is that it is a little wide since the line is doubled back on itself. Some other techniques create a smoother, less resistant connection.

One such method utilizes braided nylon to form the loop. A 2 inch piece of nylon is added by wrapping and whip finishing it to the fly line. Again the wraps should be tight to fasten the nylon to the fly line. By adding some epoxy, a strong, fairly smooth loop is formed.

An alternative to wrapping the braided nylon to the shooting head is to utilize a braided nylon connection system. The system includes a 4 to 5 inch piece of braided nylon with a preformed loop at the end. The braided nylon is hollow so that it slides over the end of the shooting head. A nylon sleeve connector is then slid over the braided nylon to secure it to the shooting head. Orvis markets a special sleeve that secures itself to the fly line. In the Cortland system, the sleeve is made of a heat shrinking plastic. When heat is applied it shrinks

down to fasten the loop to the fly line. Permabond or epoxy can be used instead of the sleeve connector. The result is a smooth, strong loop connection. In addition, it is a simple process. Packages of three braided connectors and nylon sleeves can be purchased along with instructions.

The concept of the loop at one end of the shooting head is an important one. Most commercially produced heads come with a loop, but some do not. This then requires adding one in the same manner as a homemade head. Adding a loop also applies to a shooting head that has been cut back to a desired weight. As mentioned, this is common with the Deep Water Express and Kerboom lines. The loop is used to attach the head to the shooting line using a loop-to-loop connection.

The shooting line, with its low diameter as mentioned above, is designed to glide easily through the guides and allow the shooting head to attain its distance. Shooting lines are made of either flat monofilament or level fly lines. The flat mono of 20 pound test works best for deep sinking shooting heads since this line will sink better with the head. It is important to use a monofilament designed for this purpose; that is, one that does not retain a memory of the coils of the spool after being stretched out. A limp line will be much easier to work and will shoot further. Either Sunset Amnesia or Cobra manufactured by Cortland works well. Low diameter level fly lines also have their place and work best with floating or lower sink rate shooting heads. Both Orvis and Scientific Anglers supply this type of line.

The loop on the monofilament shooting line can be easily formed by tying a perfection loop. The loop should be large enough to fit over a coiled shooting head. Such a loop will allow for an easy change from one shooting head to another. The loop on the level fly line can be formed using the same techniques as discussed for adding a loop to a shooting head. This loop should be large enough to fit over a coiled shooting head. The shooting line can also act as the principal fly line.

In this situation, the leader is attached directly to the shooting line, and by adding weight to the leader to further load up the rod, the fly can be cast great distances. This is an effective approach when fishing deep pools where backcasting is impractical or impossible. This method will be discussed in greater length in chapter 5.

Another line which the Great Lakes fly fisher will find useful in a number of situations is the Teeney Nymph Line. Although it is basically a sink-tip line, the concept behind it puts it in its own class. It is essentially a cross between a sink-tip and a shooting head. The tip section is made from Deep Water Express blended to a low diameter floating line. The result is a line easy to use and that gets the fly down to the fish even in heavy water. It is a good line for the angler fishing deep or heavy water who dislikes adding lead to the leader or where adding weight to the leader is prohibited.

Another item worth mentioning is the mini-tip. These are homemade creations using the same lead core line as the shooting heads. They are formed in the same manner as the homemade shooting heads except they are smaller. The angler should carry mini-tips ranging from 1 to 6 foot lengths. The purpose of the mini-tip is to add it to the tip section of a sink-tip or sinking line to increase its sink rate and depth. The mini-tips are added utilizing a loop-to-loop connection. The connection process for the mini-tip is discussed further in the leader section in this chapter. When fishing water where the depth and current speed

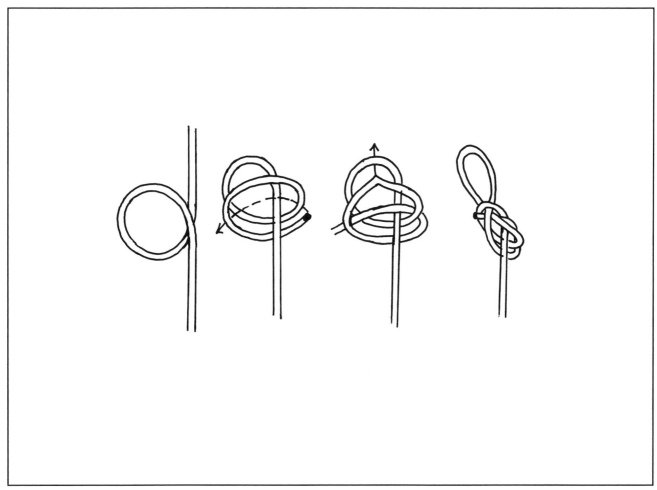

The perfection loop.

varies significantly among different pools, a simple change of the mini-tip changes the line's sink rate. Commercially tied mini-lead-heads in 1, 2 and 6 foot lengths are also available from Orvis.

A discussion of lines would not be complete without a mention of line tapers. The taper relates to the line's basic design, specifically the diameter of the line throughout its length. There are four commonly referred to line tapers: level, double taper, weight forward and shooting taper. The level line, as its name implies, has a consistent diameter. A poor casting line, this design is best for the floating shooting line or the lead core shooting head.

The double taper has a level midsection and equally tapers down to a finer diameter at each end. It is a good design for short to moderate casting distances, and it picks up off the water easily. Although most of the line types previously discussed can be found in the double taper design, the most common are the full-floater or full-sinking line.

The weight forward line also tapers down to a finer point at each end, not equally like the double taper. In the weight forward, the larger diameter section of the line is shifted toward the tip, giving it more weight toward the front of the line. This characteristic allows it to cast greater distances than the double taper. This is the common design for most sink-tips and full-sinking lines. A full range of floating weight forwards is also available.

The shooting taper is essentially the equivalent of the shooting head. It refers mainly to the length of the fly line, since the shooting head can actually be designed from any of the other three

---

Chart of Line Tapers

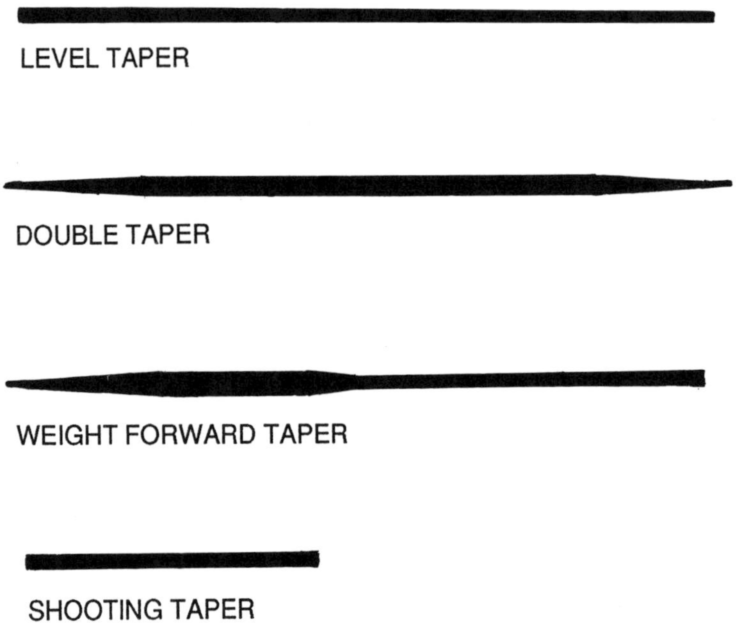

LEVEL TAPER

DOUBLE TAPER

WEIGHT FORWARD TAPER

SHOOTING TAPER

tapers discussed. Level shooting heads seem to perform better than tapered ones when compared to each other in casting and sinking ability.

There are many lines from which to choose. The choice will be influenced greatly by the water to be fished and the technique needed to effectively fish that water. Each line on the shelf of your favorite fly shop or in a catalog has its own description. This description process is a standard among line manufacturers. It is a three symbol system. The first describes the taper, the second refers to the line weight and the third relates to the line type. For example, if a line is a DT-9-F, the DT says that it is a double taper, the 9 says that it will balance a 9 weight rod and the F describes it as a floater. The other symbols used for the line design are L for level, WF for weight forward and ST for shooting taper. The other symbols used for the line type are S for sinking and F/S for sink-tip. There are essentially three manufacturers which supply a wide range of fly lines: Cortland, Orvis and Scientific Anglers.

For a complete discussion of lines, a look at fly line backing is essential. Backing is the line which attaches to the fly reel spool and connects to the fly line or shooting line. The backing is attached to the reel using the perfection loop and to the fly line or shooting line using a nail knot. Backing is generally made of a braided dacron which is manufactured for this purpose. 20 pound is sufficient for almost all situations in the Great Lakes. The dual purpose of the backing is to fill up the spool and to provide enough line to fight a fish which makes long runs for freedom.

LEADERS

My preference is to attach a short piece of .021 inch leader butt material, using a nail knot to the tip of each fly line. A loop is formed at the end of the butt section using the perfection loop. The leader is then added using the loop-to-loop connection. For floating lines, 6 inches of fluorescent orange monofilament works best as the butt loop section. The orange acts as a strike indicator to help detect takes when dead drifting the fly. When it comes to leaders, it is best to keep it simple. For floating lines, leader lengths range from 7 to 15 feet. In general, the deeper the water being fished the longer the leader needs to be to effectively utilize the floating line. Most situations require a 9 to 12 foot leader.

Most of the leaders required for this type of fishing can easily be tied using the surgeon's knot to connect the sections. The blood knot also works well for this purpose. These leaders are usually comprised of only three or four sections including the tippet. Well balanced leaders for accurate casting are tapered more gradually than these leaders. The objective of these leaders is to get the fly down and maintain a drag-free float. A typical 10 foot leader based on this system would be tied as follows: butt section–12 inches of .021 inch diameter leader material (3 to 6 inches of this portion will be the looped section attached to the fly line as discussed), second section–24 inches of .013, third section–48 inches of .011, .010 or .009 and tippet section–36 inches of 0x to 4x depending on fishing conditions. To create a leader of a different length, simply expand or shorten the first three sections of this 10 foot leader proportionately. The tippet length will normally be determined by fishing conditions. There will be times when the ideal tippet length may be only 24 inches. In this situation, the third section can be increased by 12 inches. The proper tippet length for a floating line leader is discussed further in chapter 5. The need may arise to use tippets of 01x to 02x. In this situation, the third section is either eliminated or is also comprised of .013 inch diameter material, basically creating a uniform leader.

This leader formula creates a leader of relatively low diameter. This characteristic assists in enabling it to sink fast and maintain a true drift. However, it is this same characteristic that can make it cumbersome to cast. An open casting loop

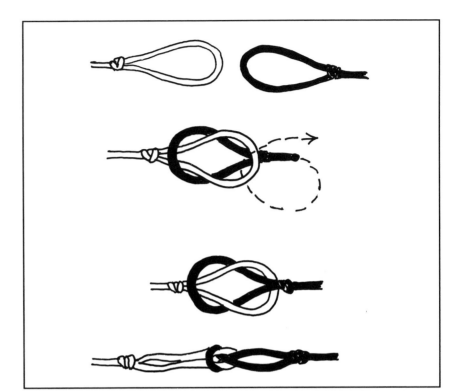

This illustrates the
loop-to-loop connection.

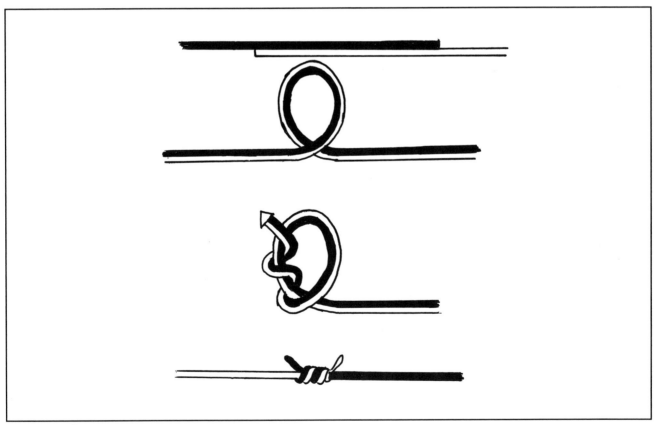

The surgeon's knot.

is the rule here and the thick butt section does help turn the leader over.

The more traditional leader formulas and commercially produced leaders also have a place in this type of fishing. There are a number of both knotted and knotless leaders on the market that will work well. Actually, gradually tapered leaders in some instances may perform better, especially when fishing shallow water where little if any weight is required. The knotless types do have distinct advantages over the knotted leaders. With fewer knots there is less chance of a breakdown in the leader, less tangle ups and no knots to hang up on weeds or moss on the bottom. These commercially tied leaders come with both monofilament and braided butt leaders. Braided butts are stiffer and help turn the fly over better than monofilament. However, what is gained in stiffness is lost in

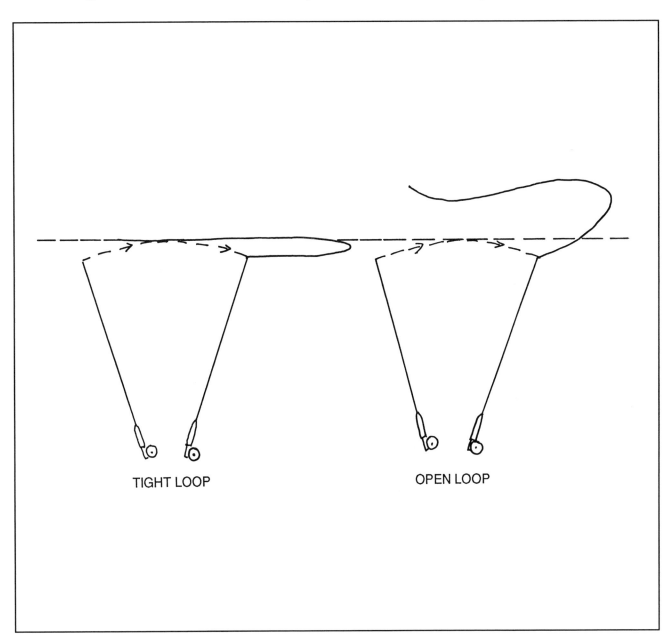

TIGHT LOOP   OPEN LOOP

An open loop is required when casting lead.

sinking ability due to larger diameter.

When it comes to sinking and sink-tip lines, short leaders are the rule. The short leader keeps the fly close to the sink source to assure that it is near the bottom. Normally the leaders used with sinking and sink-tip lines are from 3 to 4 feet in length. Such short leaders do not seem to spook fish when they are used under the proper conditions. There are some situations, such as off-color water and fast, heavy riffles, where even shorter leaders of about 2 feet can be used. Conversely, in extremely clear water where a fast sink is not required, such as in a slow pool or even on the lakes, a longer leader of up to 6 to 7 feet should be used. To use any longer of a leader basically defeats the purpose of the sinking or sink-tip line.

Keep the sinking and sink-tip line leader system simple as with the floating line system. Start with a very short butt section of .017 to .021 inch butt material about 3 inches in length finished off with a perfection loop. One of the reasons for its short length is so that the mini-lead tips previously mentioned can be added using a loop-to-loop connection. This combination then behaves as one line. This line with a mini-tip attached may appear difficult to cast but the mini-tip creates a weight forward effect and makes the line quite easy to handle for both close and distance casting. This 3 inch butt section is also added to the mini-tip.

As for the leader itself, the total length determines how many sections it will have and the length of each section. For a 2 foot leader, use a 6 inch piece of .015 inch material with a perfection loop on one end and on the other a 15 inch piece of tippet material usually from 0x to 3x. Once this is connected to the 3 inch butt section using a loop-to-loop connection, the total leader length is 2 feet. For 3 to 4 foot leaders, use a 15 inch length of .015 inch diameter material with the remaining portion of 18 to 30 inches being tippet material of again 0x to 3x. This arrangement provides a stiff enough butt section to turn over the fly and is in general thin enough to sink easily. The 6 foot leaders are tied

using 3 sections. The first is 21 inches of .017 inch diameter material with the surgeon's loop at one end. The second section is 18 inches of .013 inch material. The tippet section is 30 inches of 0x to 3x. Due to its greater length, this leader requires a bit longer butt section to turn the fly over adequately.

There are a couple of other items worth mentioning about tippets. As discussed, the normal tippet size range for floating line leaders is 0x to 4x and 0x to 3x for sinking lines. The choice of tippet size will depend on a number of factors, water clarity and size of the expected quarry being the most important. Landing fish in heavy water and in areas containing large abrasive rocks should also impact tippet selection. There are extremes when the range may need to be expanded. In situations where very clear water is combined with finicky fish, a tippet as light as 5x may be required. This is an extreme case, however. The chance of landing a trophy-size fish is greatly reduced when using such light tippets. Additionally, in order to land the fish on a light tippet, a long careful fight is usually required, which decreases the odds of a successful release of the fish. For this reason, it is a good idea to avoid such tippets. Though sometimes light tippets will be the only way to fool the fish.

There are times when tippets larger than 0x will be useful. Fishing for chinooks in heavy water is an example of such a situation. As a rule, the angler should use the strongest tippet that will effectively fool the fish.

There are a number of leader and tippet materials on the market today that provide a quality final connection from the angler to the fish. Berkely, Climax, Cortland-Precision, Dai-Riki, Mason, Maxima, Orvis, Scientific Anglers and Umpqua represents a list of most of the quality materials available. Due to constant technological innovations this list is always subject to change. These manufacturers also provide a wide range of knotless and compound leaders ready to use right out of the package.

There are two manufacturers' materials which work well for leaders for Great Lakes fly fishing. These are not necessarily the best two on the market but they possess qualities that are important to success. The first is Maxima. This is a stiff material and is excellent for the butt section of a leader. It also possesses very good strength and maintains this strength even after it has been scuffed by rocks and other underwater structure. It is, therefore, good for the middle and tippet sections of the leader. The other is Orvis Super Strong tippet material. It is very limp when compared to Maxima and has great strength relative to its diameter. This low diameter quality makes it a good choice for drag-free floating line leaders and for fishing clear water where fish can be leader shy. Because of low water absorption, it also has good wet breaking strength. Maxima appears to have much better abrasion break resistance, however.

Super Strong is good for tippets and middle sections of most leaders because of its low diameter. At times, tippet strength is more important, such as when needed for chinooks and big steelhead, heavy water or abrasive bottoms. In these situations, Maxima is preferred since its strength is unmatched. Mason leader material also has a toughness similar to Maxima. Some of the other materials mentioned above possess similar qualities to Super Strong. Climax, Dai-Riki and Umpqua tippet materials possess such qualities.

A couple of additional items related to leaders are worth mentioning. One item is sinking leaders. The Airflo and the Beartooth braided-butt sinking leaders possess extremely fast sink rates which can be a helpful addition to one's system especially when using a sinking or sink-tip line. Such leaders play a similar role as the mini-heads discussed earlier in the chapter. Due to the fact that such leaders are generally thicker in diameter, they do tend to create more underwater drag when attempting to dead-drift a fly. For this reason, adding split shot to unweighted leaders is more effective when using floating lines. The weighted

leaders may still be preferred as floating line leaders for those anglers that judge casting with split shot as distasteful. Also on the market are leaders chemically treated to sink faster and solutions that can be added to increase sink rate. Though these items do increase sink rate, the most effective approach is a floating line leader that is properly weighted with split shot or a leader that is properly balanced with a sinking line system.

Another item worth mentioning is the elastic shock leader material available on the market called Power Gum. The idea is to tie in a short piece near the tippet section of the leader. It is designed to absorb the shock of setting the hook into a monster or a fish which makes a spirited run. Some anglers prefer tying in this material near the tippet and some prefer it near the butt section. This material seems to have its best application when using lighter tippets. The elastic shock material does prevent some breakoffs in the lower ranges of tippet size. It does not seem to be critical with leaders of 2x and larger. As long as leaders are constructed out of quality material and have no significant nicks or abrasions and knots are properly constructed, breakoffs should be limited without using this material.

For the final connection of attaching the fly to the leader, the improved clinch knot works well. Use the double improved clinch with the lighter tippets.

A few final notes on leaders. To this point, when adding weight to a leader has been discussed, it referred to adding split shot. The split shots should be the removable type so that the sink rate can easily be adjusted for varying depths and current speeds. Also available are lead strips which can be wrapped on the leader. This type of weight can be added or subtracted quickly until the right amount is determined. These strips seem to hang up on the bottom less than split shot. There are two approaches for adding weight to the leader which will be discussed in chapter 5.

One last item which can be critical to

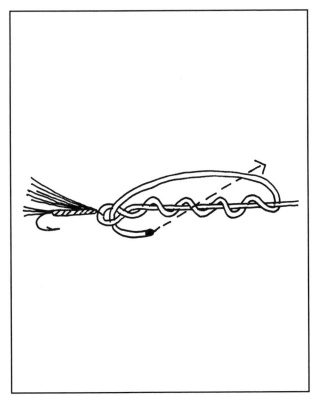

The improved clinch knot.

effective dead-drift fishing is the strike indicator. There are many on the market, or they can be easily made at home. A high floating type made of cork or foam seems to perform best. It should be adjustable, meaning it should be capable of being attached anywhere on the leader, depending on fishing conditions. A Corkie brand indicator meets these specifications. Poly-yarn can also be used as an indicator.

CLOTHING

One might not consider clothing as an essential part of their fly fishing equipment, but given some of the weather conditions faced by the Great Lakes fly fishing angler, proper clothing can figure significantly into the success or failure of an outing. Many good fishing opportunities do exist in early to mid-fall and mid to late spring when the weather can be pleasant. Pleasant weather, unfortunately, is never a guarantee in the Great Lakes region. For this reason and the fact that some great fishing action can be found in the dead of winter, it is important that the Great Lakes fly angler be prepared for some cold and nasty days.

Clothing, like the rest of the equipment related to this sport, has benefited from modern technology and has experienced marked improvements in recent years. The clothing available today is so good that the modern day fly fisher should be able to dress and prepare for whatever Mother Nature delivers.

Effective layering of clothing is the key to warmth on cold days and requires a sound foundation. This foundation is the underwear worn next to the angler's skin. This should not only have a warmth value but should be able to wick away moisture from the skin to a second layer of absorbent material. There are a number of synthetic materials on the market, such as polypropylene, which possess this wicking ability. Also available on the market is two-layered underwear which has a synthetic inner layer or a layer of natural fibers with wicking qualities and a moisture-attracting outer layer. This outer layer is either made from synthetic material or wool.

For a second layer, either cotton or wool is recommended. Both attract moisture, which is a key element of the second layer. However, wool is a warmer material and maintains excellent warmth value even when damp or wet. This makes wool the choice for the cold days. Wool is also a good choice for the next layer for additional warmth if needed. A usual arrangement of clothing for a cold day of winter fly fishing is two-layered underwear, both top and bottom worn next to the skin. The next layer is a cotton or wool shirt depending on the severity of the cold. A wool sweater makes a good third layer. When purchasing such a sweater, be sure it is a large size to fit comfortably over the other layers. For the bottoms, a pair of cotton sweat pants are the most comfortable. Cotton jeans are also adequate, with wool pants providing maximum warmth.

A good outer layer for this type of fishing is a shell made of fleece. This is a warm and comfortable material. Additionally, there are a number of hybrid fleece materials available which combine warmth with the ability to transfer body moisture to the outside. These jackets are also somewhat waterproof and if they do become wet, can be simply wrung out or shaken dry.

However, when the moisture gets heavy in the form of rain, freezing rain or snow, or a chilling wind is howling down the river, a waterproof hooded rain or weather shell is a must. A light nylon shell is usually sufficient to keep the chilling wind and moisture out. Goretex is possibly the best material available for this outer protection, and a shell made of Goretex is perfect for extreme weather conditions. However, Gortex is quite expensive. One feature to look for in an outer shell is elastic around the sleeves and hood to further prevent the advance of the elements.

To stay completely warm and comfortable, it is important to take proper care of the body's extremities. In cold weather a hat should be worn since 60 to 80 percent of the body's heat is lost through the head. Wool again is a good choice. Goretex and Thinsulate combination hats also work well. There should be no excuse for cold feet.

This angler is fully prepared for cold weather fishing.

41

Next to the feet should be worn polypropylene socks with a layer of wool socks over them. Combine this with some of the waders that are available on the market today and feet should be kept toasty in even the coldest of conditions. High warmth materials such as Thinsulate have been added to conventional waders to create an effectively insulated boot. However, the material that has revolutionized cold water wading is neoprene. It has great insulation value. Neoprene waders are available in both stocking foot and boot foot. Stocking foot neoprenes with properly fitting wading shoes are adequate for most cold situations, but the insulated boot foot types combined with a heavy neoprene are the ultimate wader for cold conditions.

A pair of the various stream cleats for the bottom of the boot or wading shoe when winter fishing should be seriously considered. Cleats prevent slipping on both streamside ice and slippery river bottoms and can be added even if the waders have felt soles. Felt soles are not as effective in very cold conditions since the water absorbed by the felt can freeze making the soles themselves quite slick.

The importance of keeping the hands warm is obvious. While most anglers would like to be able to fish without the restriction of gloves, there are some whose hands can only tolerate so much exposure to the elements. At this point, gloves become a necessity for comfort and effective fishing. Actually, once the angler becomes accus-tomed to fly fishing with gloves, it will be found that both the line and rod can be handled easily.

A solution for those who do not enjoy full gloves are the fingertipless type. These are made of wool or bunting, and while keeping the hands warm, the fingertips are exposed so that the angler has the use of the fingertips as if he or she were wearing no gloves. Such gloves are sufficient in moderately cold temperatures. When it gets frigid, the angler may prefer a full glove. The angler has wool, neoprene and Thinsulate lined Goretex gloves to chose from. All keep the hands warm and enable the angler to operate fly fishing gear. Neoprene gloves are fully waterproof and there are those available which have slits in the thumb, index and middle finger which give the angler the option to use them like a fingerless glove. Wool still keeps the hands warm when wet but not as effectively. The Thinsulate lined gloves are a good choice for the coldest days even though they are a little more cumbersome to use.

One last piece of equipment that is very important when it comes to this type of fishing and, indeed, to all types of fly fishing is a pair of polarized sunglasses with ultraviolet light filter. Not only do they protect the angler's eyes against the sun's harmful rays, but they also assist in cutting glare which is essential for the effectiveness of some of the Great Lakes fly fishing methods and for spotting fish. Both full frame and clip-on types are available.

CHAPTER 4

The Water

The type of streams and rivers which feed the Great Lakes are varied. Some of these are small creeks, others are roaring rivers, while most fall somewhere in between. They vary not only in size but also in length and in physical makeup. One thing that is common to nearly all the tributaries is that each has its own unique character and beauty.

Most of these tributaries receive consistent runs of fish, while others do not. Factors which determine whether a particular stream or river receives a good run or not include the stream's habitat, water quality, water flow, baitfish or insect life and its fish planting history. As a fly fisher fishing the Great Lakes tributaries, the ability to determine which streams receive good runs and to know which water will hold these fish may be the most important step to consistent success.

Local fishing guide books, magazine articles, and local tackle and fly shops are usually good sources as to which tributaries receive good runs. In addition, past stocking reports from state and provincial governments can be valuable information. Also, personal exploration of lesser known tributaries or those not receiving many stocked fish can sometimes yield surprising results. The reason for this is that lake-run fish will sometimes wander into tributaries even if they have been stocked or hatched in another stream or river. If the water quality is right, this can result in a self sustaining run within that tributary.

Once the angler has chosen the tributary to fish, it is imperative that he or she knows the species of fish being pursued and that species'

reason for being in the tributary at that particular time of year. This correlation may even determine the tributary to be fished. Regardless, it will certainly determine the type of water to fish within each tributary.

The term "type of water" refers to the physical makeup of a particular stretch of the stream or river. In other words, the term "type of water" relates to the characteristics of the current flow and the bottom structure that defines that particular stretch. For purposes of reading water and determining which stretches to fish and subsequently which methods to use, reference will be made to five different types of water. Each type has its own characteristics and its own value to the fly fishing angler.

ESTUARIES AND LOWER ENDS OF THE TRIBUTARY

The estuary is a term that generally is used in reference to the ocean, but it also applies here. It is essentially the area where the tributary's current meets the lake. The main characteristic of this type of water is that the current has usually slowed considerably and may be in the form of a bay. This type of water normally includes the lower end of the tributary. As a tributary runs its course, it generally gets wider and the current is slowed, and in some cases it barely moves. Lower end water is this type of slow moving channelized flow and not simply the last few miles of a tributary. Nearly all Great Lakes tributaries have some

The slow flows of lower end water can hold salmonids beginning their run and the warm water species which inhabit the Great Lakes.

of this type of water, but the length that it extends from the lake varies widely.

Estuary and lower end water is a good place to try when fish are just beginning their run. Salmonids will hold in this water before beginning their trek upstream. Many times, heavy concentrations of baitfish will be found in this water. Fish will then move into this water or remain in it to capitalize on a feeding opportunity. At this time, streamers and other baitfish patterns work well. Many warm water species which inhabit the Great Lakes can also be found in estuary and lower end water. They will be drawn to both feed and spawn. Bass and northern pike can be found here throughout the summer.

POOLS

Pools are generally characterized by water that is slower and deeper relative to the rest of the tributary. Pools will many times be the deepest portion of a tributary and will range greatly in length. This type of water will be found throughout a tributary, but generally fewer pools will be found in its headwaters than will be found lower on the tributary. More pools will usually be found on larger tributaries than on smaller ones.

Pools provide excellent holding and feeding water for both salmonids and warm water species. Fish moving up the tributaries will oftentimes rest in this type of water because of its slower

An angler fly fishing a deep pool.

RUNS

This type of water is characterized by a swifter moving current and moderate depths. Runs are usually the result of a channelization of the flow. Such a channelization can be caused by the banks or bottom structure. Runs which are created as the current flow pushes up against the bank where the stream or river curves will be found throughout the tributary. However, a higher run ratio will exist in headwaters, smaller streams and tributaries with faster current speed. Faster current speed is usually the result of a greater drop in the earth's geography.

Runs are sometimes less favored to pools for holding purposes because the swifter current forces the fish to expend more energy in this type of water. Because of this, fish like to concentrate in runs where a slower current meets a faster one. This allows the fish to hold in slower water but have the benefit of the food and protection of the

flow. Spawning fish will seek refuge in pools when fishing pressure gets heavy, since the deeper water provides a sense of security. Pools can also provide a good source of food. Fish holding in this water can expect to find slow drifting nymphs and eggs as well as minnows and other baitfish. Therefore, fish which spend a substantial amount of time in the tributary will predominately be found in pools. It is common for fall-run steelhead, which may spend the entire winter in the tributary, to be found in this type of water. When fish are located in the pools, many times they will either be concentrated near the end of the pool or at its head. Fish on the move up a tributary will stop to rest at the end of a pool after swimming through heavy water or at its head before continuing their journey. Fish holding in the tributary can also be found at the head of a pool where the current flows in, bringing with it a supply of food and a greater concentration of oxygen.

Typical seam water.

A fly fisher casts to spawning salmon in a heavy riffle.

heavier current. A piece of water such as this can be identified by the visible seam on the water's surface.

If a run has a gravel bottom and a swift current, it can be ideal spawning water and chances are it will hold fish when the time is right.

RIFFLES AND FLATS

Riffles are defined as swifter current moving over a relatively shallow, rocky bottom. This gives the water a rough appearance on the surface. Flats also consist of shallow or thin water. With less current velocity and/or a smoother bottom, the general surface appearance of this type of water is flat. These two types of water have been grouped together because, for the most part, fish utilize them in the same manner.

In general, riffles and flats do not represent the best holding water, though sometimes fish will hold in this water. This usually occurs in heavier riffles or when the water is off color. The shallow water can then offer security and protection.

Riffles and flats offer a great opportunity to the fly fisher. When this type of water is combined with a gravel bottom, spawning fish will normally be found there. As this type of water is usually shallow, it allows the angler to readily spot fish on their spawning beds. Sight fishing not only makes angling more exciting, but it also improves the fly fishing angler's chances dramatically.

In some instances, feeding fish may be found in riffles and flats. The most common occurrence of this is when steelhead or browns position themselves below spawning salmon. Their intent is to feed on loose floating eggs laid by the female salmon. Egg patterns work quite well on these species.

When fish are on their spawning beds, there are times when they can be easily spooked. Even though salmonids can appear so intent on spawning that nothing would spook them, sometimes these fish are as wary as a spring creek trout. Spawning fish are less spooky in heavier riffles than in thin flats since the riffles offer more protection and will be found in this heavier water when fishing pressure is high. Additionally, when spawning fish are in the spookier mode, they will push their spawning activities toward evenings and mornings. Actually, what happens is that they begin to set up in the evenings and continue to set up during the night and still be on the beds at first light of the following day. Good bedding water is usually near a deeper pool or run where a pressured fish can easily retreat. Clear water, sunny skies and angling pressure appear to make the fish gear their spawning rituals to these lower light periods.

To those anglers who may find fishing to spawning fish distasteful, the following points should be kept in mind. Some tributaries do not have sufficient water quality to support natural reproduction and are supported solely by stocking programs. Fish in these tributaries still go through all the phases of spawning. On the other hand, a large number of tributaries do support reproduction. It is an accepted fact that a fish hooked in such a stream or river and that is carefully played out and released will spawn again. This is supported by the fact that the runs in a number of Midwestern tributaries are supported by reproduction alone, even where angling pressure is high. The impor-

tant thing here is careful release since dead fish definitely do not spawn.

EDDIES

An eddy is defined as a flow of water contrary to the main current. Also grouped into eddies is any type of water that breaks off from the main current so significantly that the result is little or no current. This is usually created by an eroded bank, irregular bottom structure or a back slough. Most tributaries will contain some eddies. Some will be very pronounced in appearance and others only slight. Learning to identify such water can be important to the angler's success.

Eddies represent good holding water for fish. The slow currents of such water offer the perfect resting place for moving fish, especially when the tributary consists of heavy flows. Baitfish are also attracted to the slower currents of the eddy and can be found in heavy concentrations at times. The contrary or slower currents accumulate other food sources such as nymphs and spawn. Since this type of water is likely to provide a consistent food source, it is a good place to locate feeding fish.

Many times eddies will have silted bottoms since they are out of the main current flow. If the angler is able to find eddies with gravel bottoms, spawning fish may be found if the timing is correct.

Some water will be a combination of the types discussed. Being able to identify the key characteristics of the different types is the important thing and represents the foundation for successful fly fishing in the Great Lakes tributaries.

In general, the bigger the tributary is, the more difficult it is to decipher the different types of water. At first, a big river may look like just one big flow of water. After careful observation and experience on that river, however, the angler will begin to recognize pools, runs, eddies and spawning gravel that, at certain times of the year, hold a greater concentration of fish than the rest of the river.

The slow current of eddies often offers the perfect resting place for moving fish.

VARYING CONDITIONS

Much of the discussion surrounding the type of water has centered around why, when and where fish will be found. This is because as fish enter the tributary there are certain factors which impact their positioning. Under normal conditions, the guidelines discussed above are accurate. As conditions change, a greater understanding of these factors may be required to consistently find fish.

Usually, the ultimate need or urge for fish in the tributary is to spawn. Spawning fish can be easy to find at times. The spawning urge can be so great that it forces all other factors to take a back seat.When the act of spawning is not in full gear, other factors of positioning have predominate importance.

Security, current resistance, optimum temperature, food and water clarity affect positioning in the tributary. The importance of these factors will vary under different circumstances. In any case, except for periods of intense spawning action, security will be the most important. Fish will seek out water where they feel comfortable. In low, clear water such places may be limited. The deepest pools and water with a broken surface will provide such security. Often fish in low, clear water will be found positioned tight against a fallen tree, a log jam or some similar type of structure in the water. If such water provides the opportunity to get out of heavy current flows, provide a tolerable water temperature and even provide some food, fish will seek out such a place. Food can be the least important positioning factor for some species. For example, the Pacific salmon have little to no interest in actual feeding once they enter the tributary to spawn.

Under high and dirty water conditions, the importance of the factors will change. Due to the fact that the water is dirty and visibility is only a few inches, security can be found almost everywhere. The emphasis is now on getting out of the main current and finding clearer water if possible. Finding less current flow allows the fish to expend less energy. Clearer water provides less irritation to its gills. Under such conditions, fish will normally be found out of the main current flow. Water tight to the banks, slow eddies, the slow current of the inside of a bend and the slow side of a seam in a run or riffle will be the areas that fish will occupy. Fish may be found in shallow water or in water that was part of the shoreline before the water rose. Fish may also seek out clearer streams that run into the main tributary. If such water can provide security and is running at a tolerable temperature, it may satisfy all of a fish's requirements under such adverse conditions.

Water temperature can be a positioning factor which is very important at times. It can be one of the factors that trigger a run. Temperature will have its greatest effect on fish such as steelhead which spend the most time in the tributary. Browns and other species which occasionally win-

ter in the tributaries will also be affected. If water temperature drops dramatically, possibly caused by snow run off, fish will normally seek out warmer water. This may be found on the lower end of the tributary, away from the source of cold. Fish in tributaries, especially steelhead, will usually seek out the warmest water, while staying within the parameters of the other positioning factors.

The most important aspect of temperature is that it can be the factor which controls how active the fish are. Even a slight rise in temperature can get steelhead readily feeding in the dead of winter or can intensify the spawning run. Since it takes most of the day for the water to warm, the afternoons are most likely to provide an opportunity to find active fish. In the coldest winter conditions–in other words, water that is near 32 degrees F–the angler will normally find fish in water with the least current flow. Steelhead will be found in lower end water, deep pools having little current near the bottom and the slow inside edges of seam water.

Other weather conditions will also impact a fish's position in the tributary. Sun, clouds and rain can be important factors. In clear water, fish will be less wary with an overcast sky as the clouds will provide some security. Fish may be found in fairly shallow water all day, especially during spawning. Conversely, sunny skies combined with clear water create a greater need for protection and may force fish to seek out water possessing a higher degree of security, especially when pressured. Spawning fish can be found in clear, shallow water on sunny days, but generally spook easier. In high, dirty water the effects of sun and clouds are basically insignificant.

Rain can be a factor which gets fish to move. Provided that rain is not so heavy that it results in dirty water, fish may move all day. They will stop to rest in areas that provide a slow current, such as pool tail-outs, eddies and the slow side of seam water. They also can be aggressive and take flies well under such conditions. While trying to determine the spots to fish while fish are on the move, the angler should keep in mind that the fish will normally select the path of least current resistance.

Since fish will position themselves in shallow water as discussed, it is important to think before wading. All possible holding water should be fished. It is a good rule to work any water that could hold fish before wading it to get to other water. In all situations the angler should wade as carefully and quietly as possible so as not to spook any holding fish.

LAKE WATER

One other area of water that requires discussion are the lakes. As mentioned in chapter 2, good fly fishing opportunities exist in the lakes in the areas near the tributaries. As with other fishable waters, the key to consistent success is an understanding of the water.

Fish can be found near the mouths of Great Lakes tributaries almost year-round. As noted throughout chapter 2, the best time to pursue

Bank-full conditions such as these will have a significant impact on the positioning of the fish.

Locating fish in the lakes can pay big dividends.

salmonids with the fly rod in the lake is in the spring. The fall has its opportunities, especially for chinooks and browns. These species can be found close to shore as they begin their run and will readily take a fly. Summertime action near the mouths is restricted primarily to warm water species as the salmonids have moved on to deeper and cooler water. Action during the winter can be surprisingly good when ice-free water exists.

When it comes to fishing the lake, there are a few options. A good area to cast a fly is where a tributary dumps into the lake. Fish will often hold right on the edge of the flow that extends into the lake. This is a favored spring feeding area. Another area that produces consistent action in the winter and spring is warm water discharges. Such discharges are usually created by one of the many energy generation plants located along the shores of the Great Lakes. Areas that attract baitfish will often provide good action. Schools of baitfish will sometimes be located near reefs or gravel bars.

Finding the warmest or optimum temperature can be an important piece of information for the lake fisherman. In the spring, water that is a few degrees warmer than that which surrounds it can attract bait and game fish like a magnet. Occasionally, visible signs of baitfish schools will exist. Gulls feeding on or near the surface, along with fish breaking the surface can also clue in the angler.

The miles of shoreline located near the tributaries can produce good spring and fall action. Given similar conditions, some specific areas of

Fishing the right water and having up-to-date information are two very important keys to success.

the lake will produce year after year. Once located, such consistent producing areas will be a good place to start an outing on the lakes.

SOME OTHER THOUGHTS ON WATER

Other water-related items are very important. First is the need for up-to-date information on both stream conditions and the amount of fish in the tributary. The former can be gained through observation of the water; the latter can usually only be gathered from a knowledgeable angler who has just fished the tributary. It must be stressed that it has to be current information, as water and fishing conditions can vary by the day, or even by the hour. A stream in New York, the Cattaraugus Creek, is a good tributary to illustrate this variance. It is a beautiful stream, receives good runs of fish and has about 40 miles of fishable water from its dam to the lake. It may very well be the best tributary feeding Lake Erie. Unfortunately, since the stream consists of clay banks, the stream muddies quickly if there is a heavy rain or quick snow run-off. It can be running clearly one day, and high, dirty and unfishable the next.

Certain tributaries can be devoid of fish one day, and for no obvious reason, full of fresh run fish the next. Sometimes a rain or change in water temperature will trigger such a run. Most times the starting point of the run is not so obvious. Although the angler should be able to anticipate the runs of fish by such data that is presented in chapter 2, current information is going to allow the angler to maximize his or her fishing time. Obtaining this information is the key. Tackle and fly shops located near or along a certain tributary can be helpful as can area fishing hot lines. One of the best sources is an angler living near or on a particular tributary who may be closely in tune with what is going on at all times. The angler who is fly fishing the Great Lakes tributaries must always bear in mind that for the most part this is run fishing. As runs of fish can be unpredictable at times, any current information that the angler can put on his or her side may greatly increase the chance of success.

The last item is a phenomenon that has been noticed year after year on the tributaries. Spots or areas that are good fish producers in one year are normally good the following year, even though it is most likely that different fish occupy these spots each year. Such spots seem to attract moving fish. In fact, some spots are so good that if there are fish anywhere in the tributary, they will most likely be in that particular spot. Usually, such spots can only be determined through experience. Once they are known, the Great Lakes fly fisher has greatly increased his chances for consistent success.

In conclusion, it is important to emphasize that the selection of where to fish is the most critical factor for success in Great Lakes fly fishing. Spending a little extra time to find the right water can pay big dividends. Walking the tributary in search of the right water relative to the conditions can be an effective approach. Though it can take a lot of effort, the success will be worth it.

CHAPTER 5

Methods and Techniques

In this chapter, things are brought together. Up to this point, the discussions have looked at what species of fish the angler will encounter at different times of year and what type of water these fish will most likely occupy. Along with an understanding of equipment, lines and leaders, the next step for the fly fisher is to choose the most effective method or technique dictated by the situation. Once the angler develops a sound understanding of the techniques, he or she should be able to select the most effective one by analyzing the available information.

Some anglers may not be concerned about selecting the most effective technique for the situation but rather one that makes it pleasing to fish. This is certainly every fly fishing angler's prerogative and is one of the reasons that fly fishing is such a relaxing sport. Even a fisher with this approach will benefit from a working knowledge of the various methods used in the Great Lakes area.

The discussion of methods and techniques is broken down between two chapters. This chapter will discuss methods used while wading or fishing from the bank. The next chapter will discuss methods and techniques used while fishing from a boat. Some of the techniques described in these chapters are not new, but simply methods that have been developed over the years for other types of fly fishing and have been put to use in the Great Lakes area. Others have evolved to satisfy specific fly fishing situations afforded by the Great Lakes and their tributaries.

Many of the techniques used to take Great Lakes trout and salmon are different from those used to take these species in their native coastal rivers. The difference in techniques is largely the result of the difference in the physical makeup of Great Lakes tributaries as compared to coastal rivers. A more important difference may be the behavioral traits of Great Lakes fish. Steelhead and salmon in their native rivers will chase a moving fly and even rise to the surface to take one. Great Lakes fish rarely take a fly at or near the surface. They will normally be positioned on or near the bottom and except for periods of heavy feeding or aggressiveness, will usually prefer a naturally drifting or slow moving fly. Most of the techniques used in the Great Lakes area are designed for fishing a fly slowly in this bottom zone.

DEAD-DRIFT

The dead-drift is a popular method used for nymph fishing or "nymphing" for trout and bass in inland streams and rivers. It is also a popular method on Great Lakes tributaries and is best used in pools and runs. The dead-drift method can sometimes be used in eddies with sufficient current flow and occasionally in riffles. In other words, it is best used where fish will be holding and feeding, since the objective of this method is mainly to present flies in a natural manner. This is where the term "dead-drift" comes from. The fly should have the appearance that it is drifting freely with the current. The flies used with this method will usually be natural patterns representing salmonid eggs and nymphs, along with a variety of wet flies.

To attain the true dead-drift for an entire drift is not always a simple task. The term dead-drift seems over used. Many use the term simply to describe any method where the fly drifts in the current. However, this concept of giving the fly the appearance of drifting free can be critical. It brings one occasion to mind. I was fishing a tributary with a friend who is a good fly fisher. I had landed three or four lake-run browns and had lost a few others in a short matter of time while dead-drifting an egg pattern. My buddy had only one hit in a run that usually held fish. I watched his style closely to notice that he was not getting a true dead-drift but was rather adding too much tension which dragged the fly across the current. I commented to him that dead-drifting seemed to be critical on this particular day and showed him ways to improve his presentation. It was not long before he hooked fish with increased regularity.

To attain a true dead-drift, the angler will be best served by using a floating line and a small diameter leader. Sinking lines and sink-tips add too much resistance for this type of presentation. The leader length may need to be adjusted for varying depths. For the most part, a 9 to 10 foot leader will be a good starting point. In very deep pools, leaders as long as 15 feet may be required for a proper drift.

Since the fish will be most likely holding on or near the bottom, it will be essential to get the fly down. Proper weighting is critical when using a floating line. There may be times, in shallow or slow moving water, when the weight of the fly tied on a heavy wire hook will be sufficient to get the fly to the bottom. Since most good holding water has at least a moderate depth and will normally consist of a steady current flow, weight will usually be required.

Either the fly, the leader, or both can be weighted. Weighting the leader with removable split shot is preferable. This seems to provide for the best presentation, although some anglers swear by heavily weighted flies. One benefit of adding weight to the leader is the ability to constantly adjust the weight. Split shot can be attached directly to the leader. To bring the fly off the bottom for improved presentation, a 2 to 3 inch dropper can be used for the split shot. The dropper can either be the unclipped tag end of the knot between the tippet and leader or can be tied to a small two-way swivel which is added between the leader and tippet. When using the two-way swivel setup, the dropper should be lighter in strength than the leader. The other advantage of the dropper is that if the lead becomes hung up on the bottom it simply slides off and the rig remains intact. It is important to crimp the split shot down with pliers.

If the lead slides off too easily, a modification can be made. A simple overhead knot can be tied at the end of the dropper. Now when the split shot hangs up on the bottom the dropper may be strong enough to pull the split shot out. If this is not the case, the dropper should break at the knot since the dropper is lighter in strength than the rest of the leader and the overhand knot is the weakest knot. The angler simply needs to add another overhead knot and split shot to the dropper. For those who are concerned about toxic poisoning of ducks and geese that could be caused be leaving split shot on the bottom of the tributaries, nontoxic split shot has recently been introduced to the market.

Selecting the proper tippet length when using the dropper method is very important. Normally, tippet length will vary between 24 to 36 inches. The theory behind tippet length is that the weight should be far enough from the fly so as not to spook the fish, yet close enough to get the fly to the bottom. In general, when fishing slow currents and flies that sink well, a tippet of 36 inches or possibly a little longer will be sufficient. Flies that sink well are those which do not have a large surface area. Such flies are usually small and

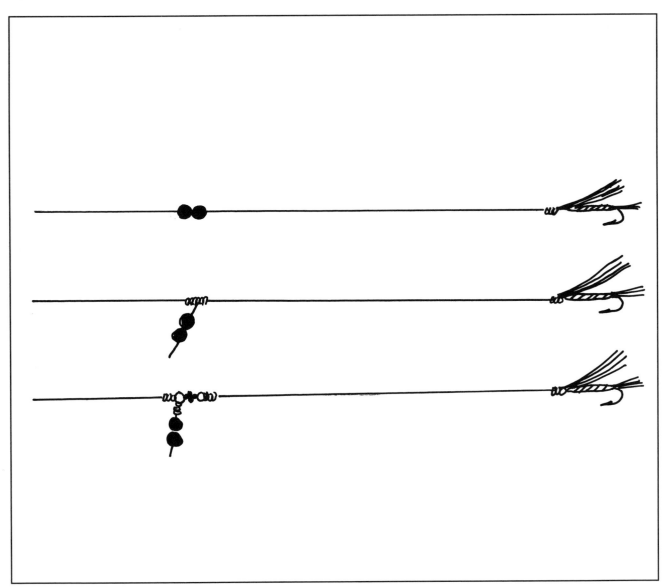

The three ways to add split shot to the leader.

streamlined. Some flies can be weighted and others sink better as they absorb water when they are fished. When fishing fast currents or bushy flies, the tippet length should be around 24 inches and sometimes even shorter. At the risk of spooking the fish, the lead needs to be close to the fly in order to get it and keep it in the fish's zone on the bottom. This is especially true in fast, shallow water and is a common condition when fishing spawning beds.

One possible solution to the problem of

spooking fish with the split shot is to paint them orange to give them the appearance of eggs. This is usually not necessary as fish do not seem to readily spook from the use of split shot. When not using a dropper, the actual tippet length does not require change. The conditions described above can be adjusted for by moving the split shot on the leader so that it is generally 24 to 36 inches from the fly.

The amount of weight required varies depending on water depth and current speed. It must be enough to get the fly down as fast as possible, but not so much as to cause it to continually be hung up on the bottom. Trial and error will usually be the way to determine how much is required. Big split shots cut through heavy surface current better than little ones, even if the total weight of the two are equal. This is important to keep in mind when fishing a heavy run. The angler should feel the occasional tap or hang up on the bottom to signal that the fly is down there. The angler should not be hesitant to add as much weight as is required for a given situation. One of the most common mistakes made by unsuccessful Great Lakes fly fishers is that of simply not getting the fly deep enough.

Some anglers are not comfortable with casting lead. It is really no problem once the fly fishing angler learns how to handle it. The angler must lower the rod tip on the back cast more than during a normal dry fly cast. This is necessary since the casting stroke, when using weight, is slightly slower than the normal dry fly cast. By dropping the rod tip further back, it allows the line and leader to straighten out completely during the back cast and properly load the rod before the forward cast is started. A slight side armed angle of the rod provides for an easier casting motion. Such an angle also allows the inexperienced caster to watch the motion of the line to improve the timing of the forward cast. Additionally, a side-arm angle keeps the weight away from the fly caster's head. The cast is completed with a level forward stroke, with a larger casting loop than used in a typical dry fly cast. It must be emphasized that it is critical that the line and leader be kept tight during the back cast and that both line and leader are totally stretched out at the time the forward cast is started. This assures that enough energy is imparted to the line to be able to carry the weight of the split shot or twist-on lead.

When using heavy amounts of weight it can be helpful to underline the rod by one or two line weights if possible. Since the weight on the leader will help load up the rod, less weight is needed in the line to balance the system. Conversely, when only a light amount of weight is used, overlining the rod by one or two line weights makes short casts easier since the extra weight helps load the rod faster.

Eliminating or minimizing drag is the key element of the dead-drift. Drag is caused by the current pulling on the fly line to a point where the fly is moved faster than or contrary to the natural current. Eliminating or minimizing drag is not easy since the tributary will be comprised of varying surface currents. More importantly, surface currents are normally faster than bottom flows. Both of these conditions tend to force the fly line to move faster than the fly which consequently pulls the fly in an unnatural manner.

To maximize the dead-drift, proper casting and line control become critical. For dead-drift fishing in most Great Lakes tributaries, the cast will be made up and across stream. The idea here is to allow the fly and weight to hit the water first and begin to sink before the fly line lands on the water's surface. Equally important is to get the fly line to land upstream from where the fly entered the water. To accomplish this the angler needs to be able to perform a tuck and reach cast. It is simply a variation of the standard cast. This cast requires the fly caster to hold the rod tip high and overpower the rod through the forward stroke of the cast. Once the line has straightened out on the forward stroke, the extra line speed added by overpowering the cast will cause the fly and weight to tuck down toward the water. This allows the fly and weight to hit the water before the fly line, which in turn allows them to begin to sink before the fly line hits the water. In essence, the fly is on its way to the fish's holding area before the current has a chance to exert a pull on the fly line. This accomplishes the tuck part of the cast.

The effects of drag can also be lessened by keeping the fly line upstream from the fly. This is the objective of the reach part of the cast which

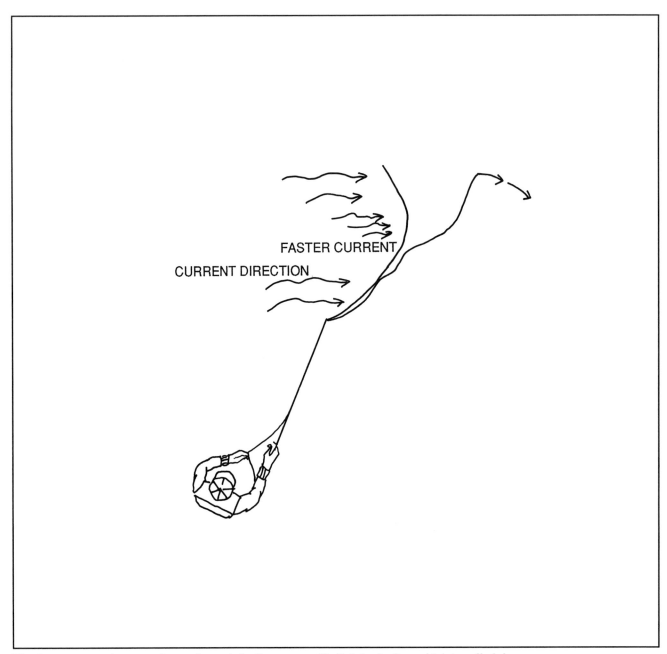

The faster current between the angler and the fly create a "belly" in the line which is called drag.

allows the fly line to land upstream from the fly and position the line in the right spot to begin the dead-drift. This is accomplished by moving the rod and pointing the tip in an upstream direction as the line falls to the water once the tuck has been completed. Depending on the current direction relative to the angler's position, the angler must either reach across or out away from his or her body in order to complete this phase of the cast. Combining the tuck with the reach may seem like too much to do on the forward cast, but with practice it can become second nature. The tuck and reach cast may be the single most important step to successful dead-drift fishing. This cast is

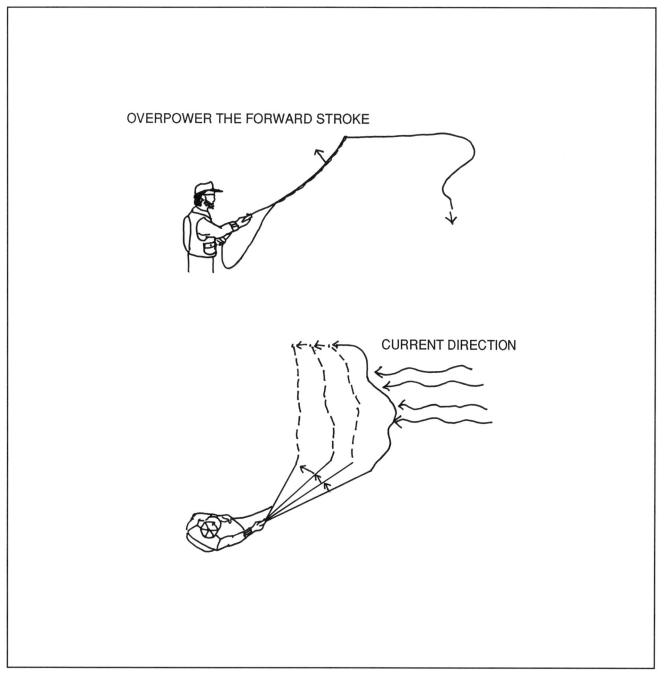

OVERPOWER THE FORWARD STROKE

CURRENT DIRECTION

This illustrates the tuck and reach cast.

a modification of the tuck cast developed by expert Pennsylvania anglers Joe Humphreys and George Harvey.

Drag can also be neutralized to an extent by proper line control. Since less drag will develop if the fly line is kept upstream from the position of the fly, the line should be manipulated in a manner to accomplish this. The most effective technique for this is mending. The idea here is to roll the belly of the fly line upstream to minimize the pull of the current on the fly. To accomplish this the rod should be held out in front of the angler

The line mended upstream to help offset the effects of drag.

with the rod tip low. The angler then must flip and roll the wrist up and outward with a motion toward the upstream flow. The idea is to move the fly line upstream without moving the leader. If the leader moves upstream in the mending process, too much power is being used in the mending stroke.

Since the current's pull on the fly line is what causes drag, it follows that minimizing the amount of line on the water will assist in reducing drag. The angler should carefully position himself as close as possible to the fish's suspected lie. The angler needs then to only make short casts. By keeping the rod tip high during the drift of the fly, only a couple feet of fly line touches the water and reduces the current's opportunity to pull the fly line. Any additional mends required should be made by a subtle roll of the wrist. The only disadvantage is that the tuck and reach cast is a

little more difficult to master when casting a very short line.

The importance of leader length cannot be overemphasized. Too short of a leader will result in drag since it will tighten completely during the drift and pull the fly out of the strike zone. Too long a leader will provide for a dead-drift, but will hamper the angler's ability to detect pickups. Experience, along with trial and error will dictate the proper length for the situation. In general, the deeper the water and faster the flow, the longer the leader will need to be. A leader length of 9 to 12 feet will be used in most dead-drift situations.

The basic strategy of dead-drift fishing is to make the cast up and across stream. The rod tip should be pointing slightly upstream at the end of the cast, and as the drift begins, the rod tip should be moved close to the water. As the fly drifts in

This illustrates the dead-drift process.

front of the angler, the rod tip should be raised to keep a minimum of line on the water and to control slack in the line. As it drifts below, the tip should be mended as required. Once the fly reaches the end of the drift, the process is repeated again. It is important for the angler to envision the mechanics behind the true dead-drift. With a proper tuck and reach cast, the fly starts drifting ahead of the fly line. As the line begins to catch up due to faster surface currents, adjustments must be made. These adjustments can come in the form of a mend or by simply lifting the dragging line off the water by raising the rod tip, whichever the situation dictates. The angler must not only concentrate on detecting takes, but must also assure that the presentation is proper.

During the drift, the angler watches for signs of the usually subtle take of a fish. Any unnatural movement of the leader butt at the point where it enters the water will most likely signify a take or that the rig is hung up on the bottom. This is why it is unwise to use too much weight since it is not beneficial to the angler's concentration or fly

supply to be constantly hung up on the bottom. To aid in the detection of hits, the use of either a fluorescent butt section on the leader or a strike indicator is recommended. The strike indicator, when properly utilized, can help detect even the softest of takes. Strike indicators can be made of foam, cork or even floating yarn tied into the leader. One that slides up and down the leader, so that adjustments can be made for varying depths and current flows, is preferable. Such adjustments can then be made in some instances in lieu of changing leader length. As with using the butt section of the leader to detect strikes, any unnatural movement of the indicator, such as it stopping in the current or a quick movement upstream, will signify a take. In most situations position the strike indicator near the point where the leader butt joins the fly line. This allows for as much leader as possible to be submerged and to maximize the leader length.

Some anglers look down upon strike indicators. They feel as though they are simply bobbers which reduce the amount of skill required to catch fish. I think of the indicator as an effective tool. When used in conjunction with proper casting, weighting and line control, it allows the angler to detect hits that may otherwise have gone unnoticed.

While utilizing the dead-drift method, the roll cast is sometimes utilized which allows an angler to fish very efficiently since the fly is in the water most of the time. As the fly reaches the end of the drift, the rod tip is raised to lift the fly off the bottom. This motion along with the pull of the downstream current will bring the fly and weight to the surface, and at this point the roll cast can be made. The tension created by the lead and fly on the water's surface will load up the rod for the cast. The trick is to end up with a tuck and reach cast at the end of the stroke. This may take some practice, but by overpowering the rod at the end of the roll cast stroke, proper results can easily be attained.

One variation to the standard strike indicator setup as described above has become popular in recent years. This rig consists of a stiff 3 to 5 foot butt section of leader. Attached to this is a 6 to 9 foot light diameter tippet section. Using a clinch knot, the tippet is tied in at a 90 degree angle. Tied in at the clinch knot is a piece of fluorescent yarn to act as a strike indicator. By using a weighted fly or adding some split shot, the offering quickly reaches the fish's holding area. A slow, open loop cast handles this rig best. Properly utilized, this setup nearly reaches the ultimate in dead-drifting a fly. It is essentially the fly fishing version of the spin fisherman's float rig, and is useful in slow, deep pools.

There is one addition to the dead-drift method that is productive at times. This entails a contradiction to the basic principle of the dead-drift method. As the fly reaches the end of the drift, it is allowed to swing slowly in the current until it reaches a point directly downstream from the angler's fishing position. There is something about this swing that entices a fish into taking. This applies even to finicky fish. The swing, however,

must be slow. The angler can attain this slow swing by minimizing the fly line on the water and by pointing the rod tip at the fly. In situations where there is a faster current lane between the angler and the fly, upstream mends may be required to keep the fly swinging slowly. Soft mends which form an "L" in the fly line will extend the drift, keep the fly moving slowly and assist in detecting takes. This works best in slower flows. In some cases, feeding out extra line will lengthen the drift even further.

The added swing technique is similar to the greased line method. With proper line control the added swing approach allows the fly to be presented slowly, which is the way that Great Lakes fish like it, and puts the fly in a position which allows for a good hooking ratio. The reasoning behind this is that as the fly travels sideways in the current, perpendicular to the fish's lie, it will have the tendency to hook the fish in the corner of the mouth. This is the area of the mouth of a Great Lakes salmonid where a hook point penetrates the easiest. A low downstream hook set helps facilitate the side of the mouth hook up.

The added swing works with all fly patterns. It seems as though the swing must impart a motion that grabs the fish's attention. This way the angler is armed with a double barrel: the dead-drift for fish feeding on free floating naturals and the swing for fish keying in on items which have a little more life-like movement. Oddly enough, even egg patterns produce fish on the swing. About the only explanation to support this is that it gives the appearance of floating eggs caught in some type of irregular current flow, which gains the fish's attention. At the end of the swing, once the weight and/or fly have been lifted to the water's surface, the line, leader and fly is in the perfect position to roll cast upstream.

The dead-drift method with the swing added is the most effective way to fish a good portion of the water found in Great Lakes tributaries. Aside from natural presentation, one reason

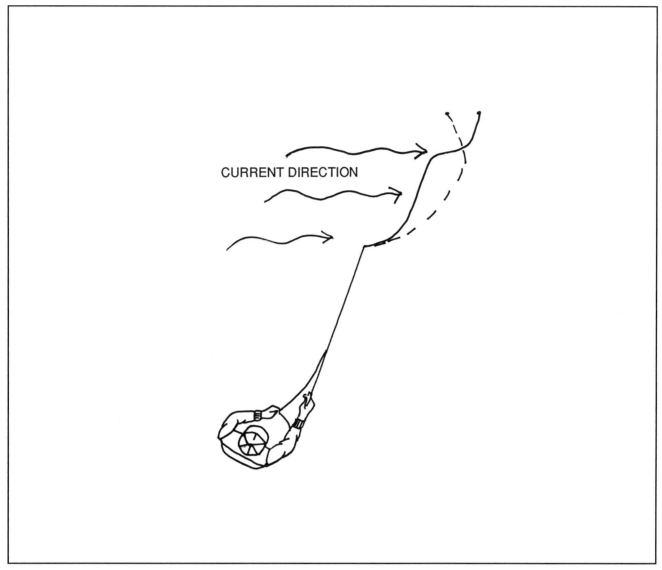

CURRENT DIRECTION

By forming an "L" with a soft mend, the drift is extended, the fly swings slowly and the ability to detect takes is increased.

for its effectiveness is efficient coverage of the water. When properly utilized, the fly is almost always in the water. By starting at the head of a holding area, making casts of various lengths, and methodically working downstream, the angler can quickly cover an entire holding area. Covering an area quickly, though, should normally not be the angler's main objective. There are times, especially when water temperatures are low, that repeated casts of the same length are required to get

a take. For this reason, the angler should work good holding water slowly.

A heavy emphasis has been put on the dead-drift method. It is a very effective method to catch fish in Great Lakes tributaries in many situations. This emphasis should in no way imply that this is the best method to use at all times. On the contrary, the remaining methods each have their place and time when they are the most effective method for a given situation.

63

TIGHT LINE DRIFT

The tight line drift method is similar to drift fishing with spinning tackle. Strikes are usually determined by feel as opposed to sight which is the key element in strike detection of the dead-drift method. This particular method is designed for short to medium casting situations where the angler can wade relatively close to the fish's lie. It is a good method for fishing runs, pools and sometimes riffles. Both floating and sink-tip lines can be used for the tight line drift method.

Lake-run salmonids will often hold in or on the edge of heavy water. A heavy run is the type of water in which to use this method. I prefer to use a floating line in this situation. The leader should be approximately 10 to 12 feet and heavily weighted with split shot or twist-on lead. The heavy weight gets the fly down through the heavy current as quickly as possible. This is important since the casts are short and, as a result, the drift time is also short.

The idea is to make an up and across stream cast. Very little fly line should float on the water. By keeping the rod tip high throughout the drift, the angler should be able to maintain a tight line and constant contact with the bottom. The angler should be able to feel the weight tapping off the bottom much the same as a drift fisher feels as the drift rig tumbles along the rocks and gravel.

As previously mentioned, the take of a fish will be detected by feel, either a sharp strike or the feeling that the fly has stopped its drift. Once again the weight added to the leader should not be so great as to continually hang the fly up on the bottom. Since heavy amounts of weight are used, it is best to employ this technique where the stream bottom is predominantly gravel. Areas that consist of many large rocks of irregular structure can result in numerous hang-ups. The angler may want to add a dropper rig as described in the section on dead-drift fishing to keep lost flies and tippet

material to a minimum. The tight line drift method, utilizing a floating line as described, provides the most efficient way for the Great Lakes fly fisher to fish heavy runs.

As previously mentioned, the tight line drift method can also be used with a sink-tip line. While my preference is to use a sink-tip in slower flows, it can also be used in moderate to heavy currents with very fast sinking tips such as the Teeny Nymph Lines. In heavier currents, mini-lead heads can be added to slower sink-tips to improve their sink rate. Mini heads are discussed in the line section of chapter 3. When utilizing the sink-tip, the tight line drift method can be used in runs, pools and riffles. Additionally, the sink-tip may be the preferred line to use when fishing this method in situations where longer casts are required.

To successfully use the tight line method with a sink-tip line, the angler should rig with a heavily weighted fly, a tip with a sink rate that will reach the bottom quickly and a short leader of 3 to 4 feet. The fast sinking sink-tip allows the fly to get into the strike zone quickly and the weighted fly and short leader keep it there throughout the drift. This provides for efficient coverage of the water. The basic technique again calls for an up and across cast. The rod tip should start out low and pointing at the fly. The angler should remove slack in the line as the drift begins so that the line is fairly tight. The rod tip should continue to point at the fly's position. Similar to dead-drifting, as the fly drifts in front of the angler, the rod tip should be raised. This picks up slack and helps to keep the line tight. The rod should then slowly be lowered as the fly drifts below the angler. Due to the weight of the fly line, a slight belly will form from the rod tip to the water which cannot be helped. The key is to reduce slack as much as possible so that a good contact with the fly can be maintained.

The angler will generally not feel the constant tap of the bottom when using the sink-tip as with fishing the tight line method using a floating line. Occasional taps and hang-ups should tell the angler that the proper depth has been reached. The take of the fish should be in the form of the feel of the stoppage of the drift of the fly. As takes are often-times subtle, intense concentration is required. A quick, hard hook set is required to compensate for the amount of fly line in the water. The hook set should be performed with a swift raise of the rod and a sharp pull down of the line with the line hand.

There is no formula for selecting the proper sink rate of the sink-tip. Each situation is different depending on such factors as depth of the water and current speed. This is the case in all situations where sink-tips or sinking lines are used. It will largely be up to the angler to select the line that is a match for the method being used and the water being fished. Keep in mind that mini heads can be used to modify any sink-tip. Based on the makeup of most Great Lakes tributaries, very fast sink-tips are most useful. Tips with a sink rate of 3.5 to 6.5 inches per second will be sufficient in normal flows and the Teeny Nymph Lines will be most useful in heavy water.

A wide range of flies can be effectively fished with this method. Egg imitations and nymphs work well, as do a variety of wet fly patterns, both flashy and dull. When using this method with a floating line, egg patterns work well. When fishing the tight line method with a sink-tip, a heavily weighted nymph natural to the particular tributary being fished is preferred.

It is important for the fly fisher to understand some of the main principles surrounding the use of the tight line method. Since the line is kept tight, this virtually eliminates the fly's ability to truly drift drag free. Additionally, when using this method with a sink-tip, the large diameter of the line further restricts the fly's free drifting ability.

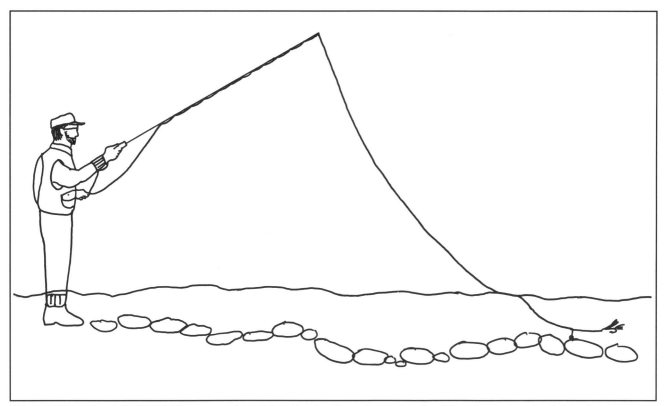

When utilizing the tight line drift presentation with a floating line, the angler should wade close to the fish and very little fly line should touch the water.

This does not necessarily mean that the tight line method is an inferior method when compared to dead-drifting, but it has certain limitations. As discussed, there are many times when Great Lakes fish are selective to dead-drifted flies and when the dead-drift method would work best. Additionally, experience has shown that when using a sink-tip, the short leader required for this method seemed to spook fish in clear, slow water on some occasions. For this reason, the sink-tip is good to use when the water is slightly off-color. Also worth noting is that the ratio of fish hooked per strike seems to be considerably higher using the dead-drift method as compared to the tight line method. It is apparent that the take of a fish can be determined quicker by sight than by feel. However, the tight line drift method used with a sink-tip may be preferred by anglers who dislike the use of weight on the leader.

UNDERSIZED LINE METHOD

I was first introduced to the undersized line method a few years ago on New York's Salmon River by expert fly fishing guide Fran Verdoliva. It is also a popular method on many Midwestern rivers. It was noted that certain similarities exist between the tight line method used with a floating line and drift fishing with spinning tackle. The undersized line method is even more similar to drift fishing. This technique was designed with the theory that drift fishing for Great Lakes fish is successful not because bait is used, but because it affords a natural presentation. The undersized line method, then, attempts to mimic the natural drift of a drift rig while utilizing fly fishing gear. This method comes so close to drift fishing with a fly rod that some may question whether it is really fly fishing. This question will be addressed at the end of this section.

As consistent with the previous two methods, proper presentation is the key consideration. This theory is clearly supported by the fact that more and more drift fishers are using flies at the end of their rig instead of bait and are experiencing tremendous results. This fact not only supports the theory of proper presentation but proves fly fishing to be an effective way to fish the Great Lakes tributaries. But enough on theory for the moment and back to the discussion of the undersized line method.

In the undersized line method, the angler rigs the fly rod with a line significantly smaller in line weight than what it is built to handle. The perfect line for this is a level floating shooting line. Such lines were discussed briefly in chapter 3 in connection with a discussion of shooting heads. Orvis and Scientific Anglers both make a line for use with this technique. These lines have a diameter of .029" and are the approximate equivalent of a 2 weight level fly line. With respect to the undersized line method, this shooting line is the main fly line. The line should be connected to sufficient backing on the reel. At the other end, a leader of 9 to 12 feet should be added. A fluorescent butt section on the leader will aid in the detection of strikes. The angler will need to add split shot either directly to the leader or by utilizing a dropper. The split shot will serve two purposes: first, it will get the fly down to the bottom and, second, it will help load the rod for casting to compensate for the light weight of the line.

The cast is made up and across stream. This shooting ability is at the heart of the undersized line cast. The cast is quite simple. The angler needs to strip from the reel a sufficient amount of line for the length of the desired cast. Since it is floating line, it will sit on the water's surface. There should be about 5 to 10 feet of fly line plus the leader extending past the rod tip. This along with the split shot on the leader will load the rod for long distance casting.

The basic cast does not really incorporate a true backcast. Prior to the forward stroke the angler holds the rod tip back at about the 10 o'clock position and slightly to the side. Ultimately, the rod tip is positioned at a point where the

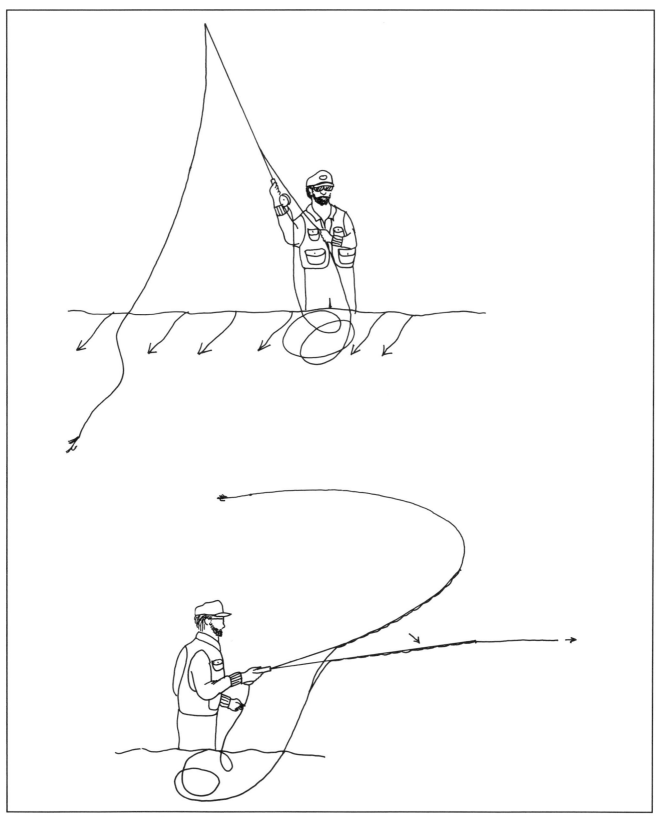

This illustrates the undersized line method cast.

line extending from the tip, including the leader, are on top of the water. The downstream current flow will help keep the split shot on top of the water. At this point the angler is ready for the forward cast. With the water surface further loading the rod, the forward cast should be a slow lobbing stroke which ideally will shoot all the line previously stripped from the reel.

Once the cast has been made, slack should be quickly gathered and the rod tip should be held high so that as little of the fly line as possible rides on the water. This will once again reduce drag. A long rod of 9-1/2 to 10-1/2 feet will assist in this. The angler should feel the tap of the bottom as the rig drifts along. Hits will be determined through sight and feel. At the end of the drift, the angler simply strips the line back in on the water's surface until 5 to 10 feet extend past the rod tip. The cast and drift is then repeated.

When this method is properly practiced, it comes close to resulting in a dead-drift. Since a tight line is maintained during the drift, some drag is inevitable. The undersized line method is best used in pools and runs, both fast and slow, where medium to long casts are required, since good distance is easy with this method. Keep in mind that long distance casts may be required in a few instances. One situation is when the angler can not physically wade any further to a holding area due to deep or heavy water. A second would be when an angler can not wade closer to a holding area for fear of spooking fish. This is common on the crystal clear streams of Michigan and other Midwestern waters.

Another advantage of this method is the fact that distance casts can be made even in brushy areas where there is no room for backcasting. Additionally, this is a good rig for cold weather steelhead fishing. Due to the lower diameter of the shooting line, it does not ice up the guides of the rod in the manner that the larger diameter heavier weight lines do. Natural flies such as egg patterns and nymphs, and a wide variety of wet flies, are a good match for the undersized line method.

For a moment it is necessary to refer back to the statement made earlier in this section that some fly fishers may not consider the undersized line method true fly fishing. For that matter, some may not even consider adding weight to the leader as falling within their definition of the sport. While today's accepted definition of fly fishing has expanded greatly to encompass many innovations, such a universally "accepted" definition does not really exist. In truth, such a definition is a topic which, at times, receives much debate among fly fishing anglers.

I will make no attempt in this writing to come up with such a definition. Such a definition of fly fishing is a personal choice. Each angler needs to have his own definition and use the methods and techniques that he or she is comfortable with referring to as fly fishing. The objective here is to describe effective techniques that utilize fly rods, reels and lines, and let the choice be up to the fly fisher as to which fall within his or her own personal definition. In light of the fact that fly fishing anglers are continually presented with challenging situations of how to catch difficult fish, certain innovations are sometimes required to catch such fish. Devising such innovations is one thing that makes fly fishing fun, interesting and satisfying. It is such innovations that will continually redefine fly fishing.

FLOATING LINE SWING

The floating line swing method is mainly designed for fishing to salmonids that are on their spawning beds. Therefore, it will be used in the types of water where spawning fish will be found. For effective use of this method, it is helpful or even critical to be able to sight the spawning fish. Sighting them does not simply mean finding fish that you can see the entire time you fish to them. Sighting also includes picking out the tell tale signs that show the angler that spawning fish are set up on their beds in a particular piece of water. Such a sign may be a female "flashing" in the water as she turns on her side and thrashes violently to push away gravel while forming a redd. A redd is a depression in the tributary's bottom where eggs will be laid. Other signs may be in the form of aggressive males scurrying in the water or even breaking the surface as they battle for position to partake in the spawning process.

Sighting or spotting fish is critical for the floating line swing method since it will directly affect the angler's position. Such positioning will in turn influence presentation of the fly. As stated previously, presentation can make all the difference in the world. The proper position for this method is across and upstream from the fish.

The floating line swing method is geared toward fishing to fish that can be seen. This will usually be in water of shallow to moderate depth and normally be riffles, flats, and shallow runs, as this is the water where spawning fish will be found much of the time. If the water does not allow the angler to spot fish, he or she is best off using a method other than the floating line swing method. Even if it is expected that spawning fish are present in a particular stretch, unless their lie can be pinpointed, the dead-drift method with swing added is probably the better choice. This is because it will allow the angler to use less lead than the floating line swing method, and it also allows for better strike detection.

The dead-drift method can be used effectively on fish that can be seen. However, when spawning fish are spotted, the advantage of the floating line swing method becomes obvious. From the across and upstream position, this method provides for great control of the fly and exacting presentation. It also imparts an action on the fly that entices fish to strike.

As the name of the method implies, the proper line choice is the floating line. The remainder of the rigging will be similar to the dead-drift method. The leaders will in general be shorter,

since a dead-drift is not desired throughout the entire drift and since the water will usually be more shallow than when the dead-drift method is used. Normally, lead will be required and can be added in the same manner discussed for the dead-drift method. For this method the preference is for the dropper setup.

Once the angler has established a position up and across from the spawning fish, the objective is to make a cast slightly downstream. Once the cast is made, the angler should throw slack into the line or make a downstream mend so that the fly drifts drag free for a short time. Ideally, the cast should be made so that the fly enters the water at a point where it will dead-drift into the fish at their eye level. Just as the fly begins to pass the group of fish, the slack should run out and the fly begin to swing in front of and away from the spawning males at the back of the pack. The idea is to play on the aggressive behavior of the spawning fish. The fish will take or chase the fly in an attempt to keep the nesting area free of "intruders." This method allows the fish to see the "intruder" for a long time and from two different perspectives: first, it is seen as a dead-drifting natural food source; second, as it begins to swing, the fly comes alive. Both presentations take fish, and the floating line swing method arms the fly fisher with a double barrel approach for spawning fish. In general, the females which are located at the head of the pack seem to prefer the fly as it drifts to them, where the aggressive males seem to strike more readily as the fly swings in front of and away from them.

When using this method it is usually best to target the males positioned behind the female. The males normally have a darker appearance. It is preferable to present the fly to the males as they are usually more aggressive. One or two "hot" females may attract males all day long. By allowing the female to stay on the bed, the angler may be able to prolong the fishing opportunity. Target the dominant male for it will be the one attempting to

Sight fishing usually requires a careful approach. Note the fish in the foreground of the photograph.

control the bedding area and normally will chase or nip at anything in its way.

It is important to note that the swing should never be fast. It should be controlled by the tightness in the fly line. The fly should swing slowly so that the fish get a good look at the fly. Takes will usually be subtle and most likely be in the form of the fly simply stopping. It is amazing how lightly a 25 pound chinook can take a fly. The angler should detect such takes by a combination of feel and watching the end of the fly line. Since leaders will be relatively short, a strike indicator is normally not required.

This method is especially effective on chinooks which so many anglers have labeled as a fish which is "impossible to catch" in the tributar-ies. It is a good method for two reasons. One reason is that it gives the fish a good look at the fly. The other is fly control. A common complaint heard from many anglers is that they do not fish for salmon in the streams because they end up foul-hooking almost every fish that they hook. The advantage here is that proper fly control with this method will minimize this problem. The fly should be cast in a manner such that, as it drifts and swings, it favors the same side of the fish as the angler. In this way, the fly will maximize the amount of time that it is in front of the fish's face. It will not be dragged across their body as would be the case if the fly was haphazardly cast across the pod of fish.

This method can provide an enjoyable way

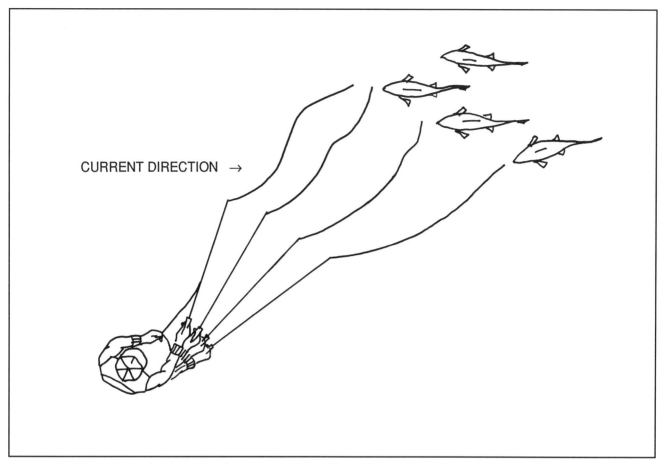

CURRENT DIRECTION →

The floating line swing method provides for great line control which allows the angler to make exacting presentations to sighted fish.

to fish the tributaries. On occasions when the fish are clearly visible, sometimes the take of the fly can actually be witnessed by the angler. For this reason, this type of fishing can generate the same degree of excitement as dry fly fishing for trophy size fish.

Since spawning fish will be found in relatively shallow water, a cautious approach will usually be required. As discussed in chapter 4, mornings and evenings can be the most productive times, and cloudy skies reduce the chance of spooking fish. On sunny days, the angler should try to be positioned so that he or she is on the same side of the fish as the sun. The bright sun shining into the fish's eye seems to greatly restrict its ability to detect movement in that direction. Of course the angler must be careful not to cast a

shadow onto the fish. Spawning fish which are unduly harassed by fishing pressure are difficult to entice into striking. This is one of the factors that have furthered the chinook's reputation of not striking while in the tributaries. They are simply not going to strike a fly when unwary anglers are traipsing through the water spooking the fish. The best targets are fresh-run fish intent on spawning. They are aggressive and normally have not been significantly pressured.

A variety of fly patterns can be used with the floating line swing method. Simple bucktail streamers are effective on salmon and a wide variety of other streamer and baitfish patterns work well on all spawning salmonids. Numerous wet fly patterns in both bright and drab colors also work well. Maribou seems to impart life on a fly

71

which makes it especially effective. Wooly buggers are real fish catchers when combined with this technique. In some situations such as shallow, fast moving riffles and runs, weighted flies seem to work best. This water has a heavy and uniform current right to the bottom. Such strong flows and possible upswelling currents have the effect of pushing the fly off the bottom. Weighted, streamlined flies assist in keeping the fly down at the eye level of the fish.

SINK-TIP SWING

The main purpose of the sink-tip swing method is for fishing holding pools and runs that have slow to moderate current flows, and where medium to long casts are required. This method also can be modified to be used in heavy currents, in shorter casting situations and to some limited extent when fishing to spawning fish. This method is very effective for fishing a tributary at the point where it flows into the lake. The real objective of the sink-tip swing is to efficiently cover the water. It is a relaxing and enjoyable method of fishing the Great Lakes tributaries. Since additional weight added to the leader is not required, poetic, long, tight-looped casts are a common part of this presentation. This method is an integral part of the West Coast steelheaders' arsenal of fly fishing techniques. An item to keep in mind is that a completely drag free drift will be nearly impossible to attain with this method. However, the efficient manner by which this method covers the water sometimes compensates for this. Additionally, there are times when fish just seem to prefer the life-like action that this method imparts on the fly.

When utilizing this method, a sink-tip is preferred to any type of full-sinking line since the floating portion of the sink-tip allows for some

Successful use of the sink-tip swing method.

control of the fly. A line with a very fast sinking section is normally used to get the fly down fast. The Teeny Nymph Lines are preferred for fishing fast, heavy water. These lines sink fast and are manageable to cast. It is important to match the line with the water in order to get the fly on or near the bottom, and keep it there for as long as possible. It is not necessary to own a half dozen sink-tips in order to accomplish this. Mini-tips come into play here. An angler with a range of mini-tips should be able to modify his or her sink-tip so that the proper rate can be attained.

In order to effectively use the sink-tip swing method to cover a pool or run, or a riffle or flat, the angler should begin at the head of the piece of water and be positioned on one side of the water, wading up to a depth that could reasonably be expected to hold fish. The angler should strip a short length of line, approximately 15 to 20 feet, from the reel. The cast should be made across and downstream. The fly will begin to drift with the current and then should swing slowly across the current. The swing speed will be controlled by proper upstream mending of the fly line. The fly fisher should strive to maintain as slow a swing as possible, especially in cold water conditions. The swing should be allowed to continue until the fly hangs in the current directly below the angler. The fly should be allowed to sit there a few seconds. Some nice fish can be taken at the very end of the swing. After the swing has been completed, another 5 feet of line should be stripped from the reel and the process repeated. This should then be repeated until the width of the water has been covered.

At this point the angler should keep the same line length and take one step downstream, and make a cast. He or she should continue this process to the end of the piece of water. This will effectively cover the entire piece of water. If not

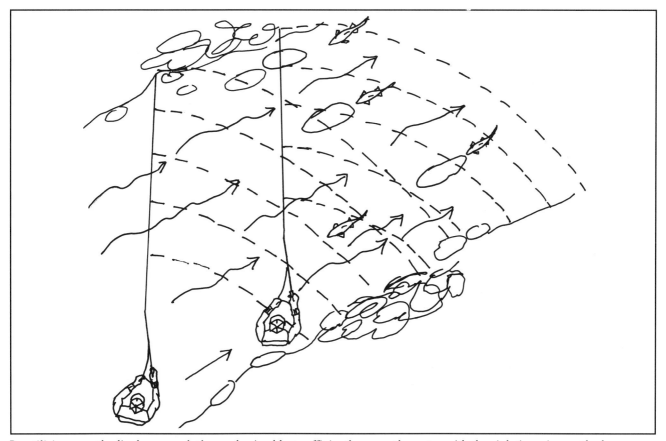

By utilizing a methodical approach the angler is able to efficiently cover the water with the sink-tip swing method.

in a hurry, or if there is only a limited amount of water to fish, make two or more casts of each length and from each position. Proceed in this methodical manner especially when there are fish in a particular stretch that are just sluggish. Such sluggishness can be caused by such factors as cold temperatures and low barometric pressure. It is in these times when repeated casts can coax reluctant fish into taking.

Strikes will generally be subtle. The angler should use both sight and feel to detect the takes. Sometimes it seems to take an extra sense. Total concentration is essential.

As for flies, a wide range of wets will catch fish. Both traditional trout and salmon flies and gaudy Great Lakes specials are an effective combination with this method.

RETRIEVE

The retrieve method can be used in various types of water and in a number of different situations. The main objective is to add a life-like swimming motion to the fly by retrieving line utilizing both the line hand and the rod hand. This is an excellent method to use in the very slow moving lower end or estuary water of a tributary, or fishing the surf along the shorelines of the Great Lakes where there is little to almost no current flow. As this method compensates for this lack of current, it is the main technique to use while fishing the lakes.

This technique is most useful for casting to fish that are actively feeding on baitfish. There are occasions when schools of various baitfish such as smelt, alewives, shad, and shiners congregate at the mouth of a tributary or actually make a run up it. These conditions can exist in the spring or fall, most commonly existing in the spring. Baitfish schools can also be found during the winter in various warm water discharges. Always look out for such conditions. The tell tale signs are baitfish

flashing or jumping out of the water as they flee their predator, fish flashing or even breaking the water while in pursuit of their meal or a fish taking a baitfish near or off the surface. When the feed is on and the angler has a pattern that reasonably mimics the natural baitfish, the action can be very exciting.

A range of lines can be used for the retrieve method from floating and sink-tips to full-sinking lines and even shooting tapers. The line should be matched with the desired depth, taking into consideration any current flow. Leader length will vary depending on the type of line used and water conditions. The basic rule still applies–longer leaders for floating lines and shorter ones for sinkers. Weight can be added for extra depth if needed.

The cast should be made across and upstream. The line plus any weight which may be added should get the fly to the desired depth quickly. To some degree the depth can then be controlled by the speed of the retrieve. In general the retrieve should be made so that the fly travels perpendicularly to current flow. In heavy current the fly may begin to swing as the flow of the water puts a downstream belly in the fly line. This is fine as long as the speed of the swing is kept as slow as possible by upstream mending. When using this technique in the lake, the idea is to retrieve the fly through suspected areas by making the cast across that area and retrieving it through. Areas to fish in the lakes are discussed in chapter 4.

Another use for the retrieve technique that can be very effective entails a slow upstream retrieve. It works best on sluggish fish which need some extra coaxing. It also works on spawning fish. For this version of the retrieve method, the angler should take a position at the head of a pool, run or riffle. A cast should be made angling downstream. The fly should be allowed to swing so that it is directly below the angler hanging in the current. If the current is strong, extra weight may be required to keep the fly near the bottom. The idea here is to move the fly slowly back upstream. The angler should retrieve the fly a couple feet and then let it sit in the current for a few minutes, and then repeat the process. After the water has been adequately worked from one position, the angler should slowly work downstream. This method allows the fish to see the fly for a long time and many times entices or enrages a fish into taking. It is similar in principle to running plugs, a technique used by many drift boaters on the West Coast and Great Lakes tributaries. This is a good technique to use when other methods fail to produce.

The actual retrieve is a relatively simple process. The line should be pinched by the index finger and the thumb of the rod hand. The line hand should then grip the line below the rod hand and the retrieve is made with a downward motion of the line hand. As the retrieve is being made, the pressure exerted on the line by the rod hand should be eased up so that the line flows through the grip of the index finger and thumb. Once the desired length of the retrieve has been attained, the index finger and thumb of the rod hand should pinch down on the line until the angler can move his line hand back up to grip the line just below the rod hand. At this point the process is repeated. The rod tip should be pointed at the fly at all times and the rod should be held at an angle that is nearly parallel to the water. There should be enough angle in the rod to cushion the strike of a fish, yet allow the slack between the rod tip and water to be kept to a minimum. The movement of the fly should be made only by the retrieving motion and never by movement of the rod tip which will reduce the amount of control that the angler has over the fly.

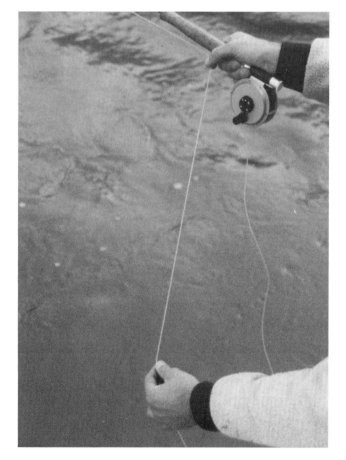

The basic retrieve process.

Some exciting action can be experienced while using this technique when the conditions are right. Hits can be hard or even jolting. This is an excellent method to use on all warm water species, especially bass. This technique is mainly designed for flies representing baitfish. A wide variety of such patterns, which represent baitfish common to the particular tributary being fished, will work with this method.

HOP METHOD

The hop method is designed mainly for fishing eddies which are characterized by a slow moving current, usually contrary to the main current. This type of water is normally created by an eroded bank or an irregular bottom structure such as a significant drop-off. In either case, the angler can usually wade close to such water or fish it from the bank. Because of this, only short casts are required to fish eddies, which makes this type of water a match for the hop method, since the fly is controlled best by using a short cast. In addition to this, the hop technique seems to add just the right action to the fly to entice a fish holding in the slow to sometimes nonexistent current flow of an eddy. The fly has to be moving relative to the bottom to consistently get hits, either through the natural drift of the current or by some added action by the angler or a combination of each. The hop method requires added action to compensate for a lack of current. This method really can be used in any

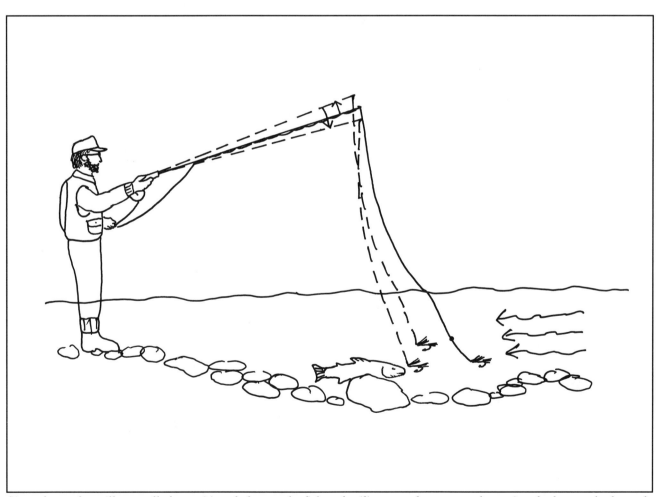

Since the angler will normally be positioned close to the fish and utilize very short casts when using the hop method, good line control can still be maintained even though action is imparted by the movement of the fly rod.

slow water situation where only short casts are required.

Either a sink-tip with a short leader or a floating line with a longer leader can be used successfully with this method. The key ingredient is a weighted fly which should be weighted toward the front of the hook. The best arrangement is to tie Lead Eyes onto the top of the hook when constructing the fly. Lead Eyes are dumbbell shaped pieces of lead that, when tied on the hook and painted, look like bulging eyes that help give the appearance that the fly is alive. Lead Eyes are similar to bead chain which is used on comet flies. However, Lead Eyes are heavier and allow the fly to sink faster and deeper, which many times is important when fishing eddies. In place of using Lead Eyes, a standard tied fly can be modified to be used with this method by simply clamping a split shot on the leader and sliding it down to the head of the fly.

The ideal cast direction for this technique is up-current. If this is impossible, up and across will due. As the fly begins to slowly drift, the line should be kept tight and the rod should be held about parallel to the water. This is also the case if there is no current to work with. The next step is to add some action. The angler needs to raise the rod tip, bringing the fly off the bottom and making it come alive. The rod tip should then be lowered to allow the fly to go on or near the bottom. As the fly drifts toward the angler the process should be repeated. A tight line should be maintained by taking up the slack in much the same way as the line was retrieved in the retrieve method. In the situation where there is no current, the fly fisher not only needs to make the fly hop off the bottom, but must make it move relative to the bottom. This is done by making the fly move toward the angler when the rod tip is raised, by raising the tip so that it angles back towards the fly fisher's position. By doing this the line moves in the angler's direction and the fly follows. Slack is gathered in the manner discussed above.

During the discussion of the retrieve method, the point was made that the action should not be imparted to the fly by the movement of the rod, yet that is exactly what is done here. This is a different situation as good control over the fly can still be maintained because the casts will be short, and in many situations the angler will be practically fishing right on top of the fish.

The movement of the rod tip can vary. A slow, methodical movement of a couple feet up and down seems to produce best. Hits can come at any time, from when the fly begins to move to when it has returned to the bottom, and they will vary from aggressive attacks to the feeling of something hanging on as the rod tip is raised. As for flies, wooly buggers and streamers tied with Lead Eyes work best. Critics of this method may see it simply as jig fishing with a fly rod. This method does take big fish, however, and critics may call it what they want. The hop method is effective.

OTHER METHODS AND TECHNIQUES

The fact that none of the methods deal with dry fly fishing may disappoint some anglers. Although I have taken a few steelhead on and just under the surface and have talked to others that have done the same, dry fly fishing is not consistent. In some instances, steelhead have been taken off the surface incidentally by anglers fishing for other species. Summer-run steelhead seem to have shown a little more interest in surface feeding. There have been a number of accounts of such fish taking a dry fly in those areas which receive runs of summer fish. Great Lakes-run Atlantic salmon do take flies on the surface, but due to the present low number of returning fish, the opportunities for this are not good. Hopefully this will change someday soon.

If confronted with a situation where a Great Lakes-run trout or salmon is feeding on the surface or where it could be enticed to the surface,

Keith Myott with a nice spring-run female steelhead.

the swing method fished on the surface with a slow swing is effective. The fly fisher may also be able to bring fish up on a standard up and across dead-drift dry fly cast when presenting natural mayfly, caddisfly and stonefly patterns.

Bass represent one of the best opportunities for surface activity on the tributaries. They readily take popping bugs, frog patterns and baitfish patterns fished at the surface using the retrieve method. Bass can be found in the lower ends of many Great Lakes tributaries. In this water, it is also possible to take northern pike on the surface. Some tributaries are host to a population of resident trout which respond very well to the dry fly. Actually, some of the Michigan rivers hold trophy size resident brown trout. However, this is not the focus of this book. In fact, volumes have already been written on how to catch these trout and the flies to use to do so.

Although this is a collection of methods

that will provide much success for the fly fishing angler on Great Lakes tributaries, it is not an all-inclusive list. Some other special methods may be needed, especially for warm water species. And while all of the above methods will and have produced very good fishing for warm water species when used at the right time, good literature already exists on many of these special techniques. In addition, some of the above techniques will need to be combined with others or modified to meet the challenge of a certain situation. Such innovation is one of the great attributes of fly fishing.

CHAPTER 6 ——————————

Utilizing a Boat

In some instances a boat may well be the most important piece of equipment the angler has. Although most Great Lakes tributaries are well suited for wading and too small to handle one, a boat is useful, and sometimes necessary, in a number of situations. These include fishing in the lake near the mouths of the tributaries, fishing big rivers, or fishing tributaries which are difficult to wade.

The point to emphasize, however, is that most tributaries do not require a boat to fish them. The angler should use some discretion on which water to use a boat. If the tributary is too small for boat traffic, using a boat will probably decrease the angler's success by spooking the fish as the boat drifts over them and at the same time make a number of enemies among the wading or shore bound anglers. Conversely, when used on larger tributaries, a boat can make available to the angler much more water to fish than he or she would have by strictly wade fishing, which in effect gives everyone more room to fish. The rule here is to use a boat when it is necessary for success and in order to effectively fish a particular tributary as opposed to just mere convenience to the angler. The objective of this chapter is to cover the proper use of a boat to improve the angler's success.

For the most part, the methods used when utilizing a boat are not that much different from what was covered in the previous chapter. A number of modifications are required in the equipment and approach. This chapter will take a look at these modifications along with examining how

a boat can work for the Great Lakes fly fisher.

TYPES OF BOATS

The types of boats that can be used for fishing the tributaries and in the lakes are wide and varied. For drifting smaller streams and rivers from one point to another and where the use of a motor is not feasible due to size or current strength, a drift boat or pram works best. Such boats are designed so that the surface area resting on or in the water is kept to a minimum. This allows for the drift boat or pram to be easily maneuvered or controlled with a pair of oars. Rubber rafts constructed for this purpose and flat bottom boats can also be used, but they are not as easy to control with oars.

For big rivers where motors are practical and for fishing the lakes, a conventional style boat of 16 to 18 feet is preferred. This is big enough to take onto the Great Lakes, even on moderately rough water conditions, yet small enough so that it is easy to control when drifting the larger rivers. Aluminum is best, as this material is more durable than fiberglass, especially against the ice flows that can be encountered when steelhead fishing in the winter. The boat should be simple, open and free of the type of obstructions that can tangle the slack in a fly line that is left hanging by the angler's feet. The boat should have some type of a floor board to make it easy to stand and thus easier to fly fish. A boat might be equipped with an inexpensive depth and fish finder which gives a readout of

The design of this boat is perfect for Great Lakes fly fishing.

the bottom structure and an electric motor. The importance of these two items will be discussed later in this chapter.

DRIFT FISHING

The basic use of a boat is essentially for transportation. In other words, it should be utilized to drift to productive fishing areas and drift through unproductive water. This technique is best used on medium to large tributaries when drifting from one point to another. Arranging for a shuttle at the end of the float is important. This can be accomplished by utilizing two vehicles or arranging for such a service through a local tackle shop. Again, as discussed, a drift boat or pram will work best for this approach.

One of the best examples of this approach brings to mind a float trip on the Pere Marquette with experienced river guide Mike Gnatkowski. It was early May and although the height of the

steelhead run had past, a number of fish remained throughout the river. The idea here was to search out spawning fish as we drifted. When fish were spotted, we tried to pull the boat to the bank without spooking the fish. Even if we did spook them, the ones that were really intent on spawning would set up again in a short time. We would then get out of the boat and begin fishing to the steelhead. In some instances, the best approach was to fish right from the anchored boat. We covered a lot of water and fished to many steelhead that day. I had many more opportunities provided by floating than I would have by wading since the fish were so spread out. Additionally, the stretch we floated would have been difficult to wade and had limited access. Although I had a tough time landing fish on this day, it was not for a lack of opportunity. This floating and searching approach is also good for spawning salmon.

The angler can also fish from a drifting drift boat or pram when fishing medium to larger

81

Utilizing a drift boat can be productive as well as providing a very enjoyable experience.

sized tributaries. The objective is to utilize one of the methods discussed in the previous chapter while the boat moves through productive water. Such water, especially on larger rivers, will sometimes be only reachable by boat, giving the angler who is fishing from one the advantage. The dead-drift method and the retrieve technique seem to work best for this approach. The dead-drift method is preferred for water that has a medium to fast current flow. The retrieve method is more effectively utilized in slow moving pools or lower ends.

When using the dead-drift method from the boat the rigging should be similar to what was described in the preceding chapter. Extra weight may be required to get the fly down fast. This is a popular method of fishing nymphs on Western rivers, but can easily be adapted to Great Lakes fishing. The objective is to allow the fly to drift naturally with the current. Since the angler is drifting with the current, such a drag-free drift is easier to attain from the boat than when wading or fishing from the bank. A strike indicator is useful when fishing in this manner. The cast should be made slightly downstream and out from the boat into any good-looking holding water. The cast is made slightly downstream since the boat will generally travel faster on the surface currents than the fly will near the bottom. The angler should watch the strike indicator to signal the take of a fish. As the boat catches up to the fly and it begins to be pulled by the current, it is time for another cast and the process is repeated.

The retrieve method, while fishing from the boat, is very similar to how it is used while wading. This method works best in the slower currents which allow the angler to properly work the fly. If possible, the person manning the oars should try to row against the current further slowing the boat and allowing the angler to work the fly slowly through the feeding zone. Casts are usually made across current, although casts both upstream and down can be utilized when the situation dictates. In very slow flows, like those found in the lower ends of tributaries and in deep pools, the boat can even be anchored and casts made in all directions. Many times good holding water exists in lower ends and is only accessible by boat. Since this type of water generally has a uniform appearance, finding such good holding water sometimes can only be learned by experience.

A canoe can sometimes be used in very slow lower end water. One advantage of the canoe is that it can be drifted or paddled to the fishing area, and if the current is not too strong, it can be paddled back to the starting point. This eliminates the need for a shuttle which is required when drifting. In areas where it is feasible, a small boat with a motor can be utilized in the same manner as the canoe.

FISHING LARGE RIVERS WITH A BOAT

To this point we have mainly discussed the approaches for moderately sized tributaries. When it comes to fishing the large rivers of the Great Lakes, such as the Niagara in New York or possibly the Muskegon in Michigan, additional modifications are required for success. When fishing these large rivers from a boat, most success will come while drifting a fly on or near the bottom as

the boat is carried by the river's current. When fishing medium sized tributaries with moderate depths, the angler can reach the bottom by using a long leader on a floating line as discussed. Unfortunately, the depths of some of the big rivers preclude the angler from using such a set up. Some of the drifts in the Niagara are 20 to 30 feet deep. The only way to effectively fish this type of water is by using a fast sink-tip or sinking line, or a shooting head.

When fishing deep like this, a 300 or 400 grain Teeny Nymph Line is a good choice. The sinking portion is 24 feet and this combined with a 4 to 8 foot leader gets the fly down to the strike zone. If extra depth is needed, the floating shooting section will also sink when it is pulled under by the sinking section. Note that slightly longer leaders can be used in this type of fishing than when using a sink-tip while wade-fishing. This is due to the fact that the drifts are longer which gives the fly more time to get to the bottom. If a longer leader can be used, it is less likely that the fly line will spook any fish.

Another good combination for this type of fishing is the shooting head arrangement discussed in chapter 3. One that sinks very fast is preferred. A shooting head made from Deep Water Express or from plastic coated lead core line such as Cortland's LC-13 works well. The shooting heads used are usually between 225 and 300 grains. When using a shooting head in this deep water situation, use flat monofilament for the running or shooting line. Flat monofilament sinks better than the low diameter fly line. Besides, if the angler wanted to fish with this type of shooting head arrangement using the low diameter fly line as its running line, the Teeny Nymph Line would be a better choice since it eliminates the connection loops. To compare the two setups, the Teeny Line is easier to control and with which to fish when utilizing a boat in deep water situations. The shooting head and flat monofilament combination seems to provide a better feel of the bottom and of strikes.

In addition to the sinking line, much of the time a small split shot is added to the leader. This accomplishes two things: it keeps the fly closer to the bottom and the weight can be felt tapping along the bottom as the boat drifts with the current, signalling to the angler that the fly is on the bottom. Since hang-ups on the bottom can occur frequently, a dropper is normally used for the split shot. Droppers were discussed in chapter 5 in the section on dead-drifting.

The cast for this big water fishing is simple. It consists of an open loop downstream stroke. The length of the cast should be approximately the amount of line required to get to the bottom. The line should then be allowed to sink. Depending on the depth, this may take a few seconds. The angler should feed out more line if required to get to the bottom. Once on the bottom, the fly drifts along as the angler and the boat drift on the surface. The angler does not need to retrieve the fly until the good holding water has been drifted through. At this point, the boat can be allowed to drift down to new possible holding water, or if the river is large enough for a motor, it can be driven back up to the head of a drift and the process can be repeated. This latter practice is the common way to fish the mighty Niagara River.

When using this deep water method, a variety of flies can be used. The most common flies are egg patterns and nymphs. When using these patterns, the objective is to attain as drag-free a drift as possible. This means that the angler

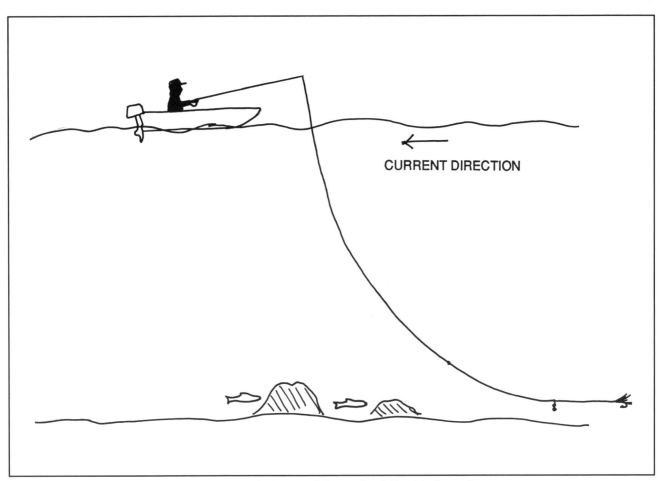

CURRENT DIRECTION

This illustrates the deep water presentation as the boat and the angler drift with the surface current.

should attempt to maintain the fly line in a position that is straight down from the boat,which is not always a simple task. Streamers can also work very well when coupled with this technique, especially when a good number of baitfish are present. When using streamers, adding a twitch to the fly as it drifts along makes it more life-like and sometimes irresistible to the fish. Strikes usually come in the form of pickups. The angler must concentrate closely on anything that stops or slows the fly and quickly set the hook before the hook is spit out by the fish. A quick set is important as the fish may already have had the fly in its mouth for a time before it is signaled to the angler.

There are times when maintaining a natural drift is difficult. This is usually the result of windy conditions. Such conditions can cause the boat to travel in an unnatural manner relative to the current flow. The result of the unnatural drift on the water's surface will result in one on the bottom, for drag is created which will negatively affect the presentation of the fly. To combat this, oars can be used to continually position the boat. An easier solution is to use an electric motor. By making periodic adjustments to the boat's position using the motor, a natural drift can easily be maintained. Anglers fishing the larger rivers with any regularity should make such a motor part of their standard equipment.

Maintaining the natural drift is very important when using egg patterns and nymphs. However, it is not as critical when using streamer

This steelhead was caught by the author while drifting an egg pattern in deep water.

85

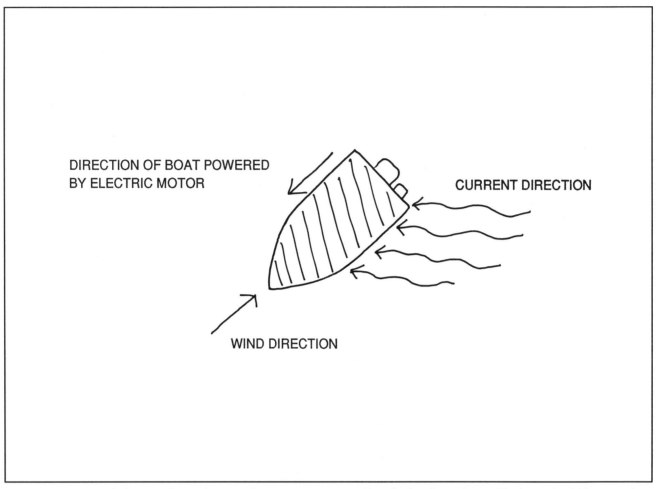

DIRECTION OF BOAT POWERED
BY ELECTRIC MOTOR

CURRENT DIRECTION

WIND DIRECTION

To maintain a true drift in windy conditions, adjustments are required to the boat's position. The boat should be moved toward the direction of the wind so that it will drift in the same manner as if there was no wind.

patterns. Actually, a little drag on this type of fly can even add some action. This technique has proven itself to be an effective way to fish big rivers for all species of salmon, trout, char and nearly all the warm water species available in the Great Lakes.

FISHING THE GREAT LAKES WITH A BOAT

The discussion in this chapter so far has centered around the use of boats in the tributaries. Boats can also be useful in the Great Lakes themselves. Good opportunities exist in the lakes near the mouths of the tributaries in the spring and then again in the fall. Although some of this lake fishing can be capitalized upon by wading at the mouth or along the shoreline, a boat opens up much more water.

When fishing the lake, a reasonable attempt should be made to either locate fish or to fish an area that should hold some. Two common ways to find fish, both game and bait, is through the use of both an electronic fish finder and the use of a thermometer. Inexpensive fish finders may not pick up game fish in all situations, but they will provide the angler with factors which may be more important, such as bottom depth, contour and baitfish schools. Locating the optimum temperature in some cases will be the most important factor in locating fish in the big lakes since Great Lakes fish constantly seek out water that has a temperature which is favorable to that species. Water temperature can also determine the areas where baitfish will be found.

The most basic approach to fishing the lakes is to fish the area where the tributary flows into the lake. Most of the time this type of water can be fished by wading or from a boat. The swing method can be used effectively in this current flow. Working up and down the shoreline and in the quiet bays utilizing the boat is also enjoyable.

DRIFTING

When the wind is sufficient to push the boat along at a steady pace, drifting through productive areas is a favored approach. This technique entails a full sinking line, shooting head or Teeny Nymph Line with a sink rate that is a match for the depth of the water being fished. The cast should be made in the direction from which the boat is moving away. Casting with the wind would be easier, but the boat would then drift over the fly and line making it difficult or perhaps impossible to control. A cast of 60 feet or so will usually be sufficient. A low, tight loop will help

In the early spring just after ice-out, some excellent opportunities exist along the shorelines of the Great Lakes.

punch it into the wind. Once the cast has been made, the fly should be allowed to sink to the desired depth.

Many times the fish will be found in 20 feet of water or less in the spring. It will not always be necessary to be on the bottom since fish will be cruising at different levels and will rise a few feet from the bottom to feed. Extra line can be fed from the reel if needed. The drifting of the boat gives the fly motion. In addition to this, if a twitch is added to the fly with a slow sweep of the rod tip extra action will be attained. Use a slow, periodic retrieve until the fly is brought to the boat. The process is then repeated. Although this is a great approach for salmonids, it can also be very effective for Great Lakes smallmouths when they are in 10 to 30 feet of water.

A variation of this approach is to drift the bays and shorelines, working the bottom with the hop method as discussed in chapter 5. In the hop method when fished from a boat, a sinking line, shooting head or Teeny Nymph Line is combined with a weighted fly, and it is essentially jigged on the bottom. This jigging motion is attained through an up and down motion of the rod tip. The weight of the fly combined with the fly line should be sufficient to reach the bottom of the depth being fished. Flies weighted with Lead Eyes enhance the action of this technique. Again, the cast should be made into the wind and at a length that approximates the depth of the water. Leader length for both of the drifting approaches should be about 6 to 8 feet.

RETRIEVE METHOD

When winds are light, the retrieve method works well when fishing the lake. This can be the best approach when fishing to a concentration of feeding fish. Such concentrations can commonly be found in the spring and winter, in warm water discharges. Other places to find concentrations of fish include tributary mouths, gravel bars and drop offs. Where it is safe to do so, anchoring the boat in a position near the concentration of fish and making repeated casts to that area is the most efficient way to take advantage of this situation.

Another time for the retrieve method is when the angler needs to fish deep. This may be required in late spring. The retrieve method combined with deep sinking shooting heads can be used to cover depths of 30 to 60 feet or even deeper.

The retrieve method should be fished the same way in the lake as described in chapter 5. The length of the cast can vary greatly. When covering the water blindly or an area where it is possible that fish will be found, the longest cast the angler is capable of is best. Such a long cast puts the fly in the water for a longer time and hence allows a greater chance for a hookup. A double haul cast enables the angler to attain the greatest distance. If the angler is fishing to a concentration of fish that are close to the boat, shorter casts may provide the more efficient approach. Leader lengths can vary from about 2 to 8 feet, depending on such factors as water clarity and the depth the fly will be fished. In general, deep sinking lines should be matched with shorter leaders. Another item to note is that shorter leaders make long casts easier, especially when fishing big flies. Big flies will be used, as baitfish patterns are the obvious choice to match with this method. Be ready; aggressive hits in the spring are common.

TROLLING

Trolling the fly behind the boat as it is powered by the motor is another method for fishing the lake. It is a simple method patterned after the most popular way to fish the Great Lakes with conventional tackle. Though it is a method that many contend is not true fly fishing, it is an effective way to take salmonids in the lake on a fly and fly fishing equipment. Actually, at times it can be the most effective method to use in the lake for no other reason than it keeps the fly in the water

Trolling is an effective method for Pacific salmon, brown trout and lake trout.

longer than the other techniques. In all fairness, there is more to this approach than just dragging a fly around.

Even though much water can be covered while trolling, it is important to concentrate this approach in areas where fish are expected to be found. A fly can be trolled through almost any of the areas in the lake which hold fish. A good sturdy rod for this type of fishing is important. Since casting is not required, a heavy fiberglass rod will work well. Holding the rod is preferable to using a rod holder. First, it enables the angler to impart extra action to the fly by sweeping the rod back and forth which speeds up the motion of the fly in order to enhance the fly's life-like appearance. Second, it allows the angler to feel the normally aggressive

hit of a springtime fish. This jolting surprise is one of the most enjoyable aspects of trolling a fly. Another way to add motion to the fly is by steering the boat in an "s" pattern. The continual turns have the effect of constantly speeding up and slowing down the fly to make it look alive.

Trolling speed is an important consideration. Oftentimes experimentation is required to find the right speed for the given situation. Too slow a speed may give the fish too good of a look at the fly. Too fast of a speed has the effect of not allowing the fly line and fly to properly sink which prevents the fly from being presented to the fish. The length behind the boat that the fly is trolled also can vary. About 100 to 150 feet is sufficient.

As for lines, a wide variety can be used.

Fast sinking shooting heads of lead core or Deep Water Express attached to a flat running line work best. Such lines sink fast and deep in still water. They are also good for shallow to moderate depths when trolling since the boat's movement flattens out the line and prevents it from sinking too deeply. Leader lengths vary depending mainly on water clarity. A leader of about 8 feet is preferred for most conditions. In cases where extra depth is required, split shot can be added to the leader or weighted flies can be used.

Some of the flies used for trolling are quite large. Since they do not have to be casted, such large flies are a good choice. Good success occurs on 2/0 tandem hook streamers. A tandem hook arrangement is more desirable than long shanked single hooks which seem to give the fish extra leverage to throw the hook free. Materials that give the impression of movement and flash such as bucktail, marabou, Hairabou, Krystal Flash, Crystal Hair and Flashabou are all good.

A few guidelines can be used to select the proper line when fishing the lakes. Weight forward lines are useful for distance casting on the lake. Shooting head arrangements can also achieve great distances and those utilizing flat monofilament running lines and heavy heads can be used for fishing deep. As far as sink rates go, however, the angler must be able to match the proper line with the conditions as discussed in chapter 5. Such factors as water depth and the speed of the drift will have a direct impact on the line selection. The angler must be able to assess the factors and make a choice based on this assessment.

CHAPTER 7————————————————

Flies

The range of flies used to catch Great Lakes fish is wide and varied. This chapter covers flies that are consistent fish producers. A list of all flies that catch fish in the Great Lakes would be simply impossible since it seems almost any combination of fur and feathers will take these fish under some conditions. Most of the time proper fly selection will be important. The selection of flies presented in this chapter have all provided above average results when used at the proper time in the Great Lakes and their tributaries. Some of the flies are tried and true patterns that have been developed outside the Great Lakes area while others have been created specifically for this type of fishing. Still others are traditional patterns that have been modified for use in the Great Lakes area. One characteristic that is common among almost all of these patterns is that they are simple to tie. This is an important consideration since flies can be easily lost while utilizing the methods that are effective in the Great Lakes area.

Actual fly selection usually is a personal choice. The angler tends to fish with the fly pattern that provides the most confidence. Fly selection should be made based on all available information. The patterns described in this chapter have been classified into four categories. These are: egg patterns, natural food patterns, wet flies and baitfish patterns. Throughout the discussion of techniques, an attempt was made to associate the types of flies that work best with each method. When it comes to fly selection there are some key considerations to keep in mind.

When presenting flies to fish holding or feeding in a tributary, it is normally a wise choice to use a fly representing a food source which would be commonly found there. Egg and natural patterns should be the obvious choice in this situation. Egg patterns may be more common in the fall and spring when a variety of species of fish are using the tributaries to spawn. Natural patterns such as nymphs might be the choice in the winter when fewer eggs are present and in the spring when nymphs become more active. Both egg and natural patterns should be used with techniques that present the fly in a natural, freely drifting fashion.

When fishing to spawners on their beds, a slightly different approach may be required. Although egg and natural patterns can work well in this situation also, a wet fly attractor might be able to entice or aggravate a fish into striking when other patterns cannot. Since such flies are normally tied with materials which impart a life-like image in the current of a tributary, wet flies are a good choice for those methods which utilize a swinging action. In addition, many wet flies are tied using colors which are similar to eggs or nymphs. Some such wet flies can then also be used with methods which present the fly in a freely drifting manner by those anglers who prefer traditionally tied patterns.

Baitfish patterns are best used in those situations where fish are feeding freely on forage fish. Some salmonids and warm water species enter some tributaries for the sole purpose of gorging themselves on runs of smelt, alewives, shad or shiners. Baitfish patterns are the obvious choice for such situations. Baitfish patterns are also the main offering in the open waters of the Great Lakes. These patterns imitate the main food source for the fish while in the lake. Baitfish patterns can also be used as attractors when fished in the tributaries. Many spawning fish have been agitated into striking by a brightly colored streamer. They can also be used as natural patterns when only a few actual baitfish exist in the tributary.

The size of the flies used vary with the conditions. As a general rule, low and clear conditions usually dictate the use of small flies. Fish that have been exposed to heavy fishing pressure also react better to smaller flies. Larger flies are usually used to the angler's advantage in high and stained water.

Color can be a key factor in fly selection.

Obviously, when fishing natural patterns, the color of the fly should approximate that of the food source which is being imitated. As for egg patterns, one theory suggests that brighter colors be used in the fall and spring when fishing near active spawning beds. The bright color represents fresh eggs. During the winter when there is no spawning activity, washed out colors should be used to imitate eggs that have been in the water for a while. This is certainly not a hard and fast rule when selecting an egg pattern, but can be used as a guide.

When the water is low and clear, drab colors are usually a good choice. In dirty water conditions, there seem to be two schools of thought. Some anglers prefer bright flies in these conditions since it is felt that these colors will show up better in such water. Others prefer dark colors based on the premise that dark casts a better silhouette in water of low visibility.

A collection of Great Lakes flies used to catch this trophy.

As with all fly fishing generalizations, there are exceptions. Actually, the fly selection process seems to vary by tributary. One example of this comes quickly to mind. In the pristine streams of Michigan, small naturally colored flies are the predominate choice for feeding fish. However, in some New York tributaries, brightly colored flies work very well, even in the middle of winter in clear water conditions. A much larger concentration of natural food items in the nutrient rich tributaries of Michigan may contribute largely to this difference. There are times when large flies were necessary to take fish on one tributary but where the same fly would spook fish in another.

When it comes to salmonids, their willingness to take a fly sometimes varies with the amount of time the fish has spent in the tributary. Fresh-run fish, either holding or spawning, will generally take a fly better than stale fish which have spent a long period of time in the tributary. Such fish, especially if they have received heavy fishing pressure, can become quite difficult to entice into taking a fly.

The angler should not be afraid to experiment with new patterns. When it comes to this type of fishing there is an infinite number of combinations of materials which will catch fish. Finding the right combination and creating your own flies is all part of the fun.

With regard to hook selection, my preference is for chemically sharpened hooks with a small barb. There are a number of hooks on the market of sufficient quality. Mustad, Tiemco, Dai Riki or Daiichi are good choices for standard hooks. Gamakatsu seems to produce the best egg-style hook. Throughout this chapter a range of sizes is given for each fly. Unless otherwise stated, the shank length of the hook in each range should be the approximate length of the standard Mustad salmon style hook model 36890 or the Tiemco model 7999.

Weighting the fly can be an important consideration. There is normally only a need to weight some patterns. These are basically the natural patterns used with the methods that require a weighted fly such as the tight line drift method. Generally, the sink rate of the fly is better controlled by use of split shot or the proper sinking line. When adding weight to the fly, the easiest method is to wrap lead wire onto the hook shank. Many fly tiers prefer tying in a strip of lead to the underside of the hook. It is felt that this enables the fly to drift in a more natural looking manner.

EGG PATTERNS

GLO BUG

Hook: Egg style sizes 2 to 10. Thread: Orange or yellow. Body: 3 to 4, 2 inch or shorter strands of Glo Bug yarn. The strands should be combed out with a fine tooth comb. The material is placed on top of the hook and tied in firmly in the middle. Best results can be obtained by actually tying one strand in at the top and one on each side of the hook. Additional wraps should be made directly in front of the material to secure it. The thread is then tied off. Grab the ends of the strands, pull straight up and cut all the material with a quick, clean snip with a pair of sharp sewing scissors. The size of the egg can be controlled by how close the cut is made to the shank of the hook. Stroke the yarn down so that it covers the hook shank. Trim as required.

This is the most effective single egg pattern on the Great Lakes tributaries. Glo Bug yarn comes in a very wide range of colors making it a very versatile pattern. It is such an effective pattern that if the angler was restricted to two patterns for fishing the tributaries, this would be one of them. One variation that seems to enhance the basic Glo Bug pattern is to tie it with a dot. This is accomplished by adding a strand of a different color yarn. It seems to be most effective when the dot is of a brighter color than the rest of the egg. This is a very good pattern to use when utilizing a method that presents the fly in a natural drift.

GLO BOU

Hook: Egg style sizes 2 to 10. Thread: Orange or yellow. Tail: Five to eight strands of Flashabou cut to approximately 1/2 an inch long. Body: same as Glo Bug.

This Glo Bug variation has worked so well that it deserves its own name. It has proven to be especially effective on lake-run brown trout when used with the dead-drift method. A new commercially produced pattern that also gives this flash illusion is the Meg-A-Egg. This pattern has the flash material protruding from the body of the fly and also works very well.

HANK'S SPECIAL

Hook: Sizes 2 to 6. Thread: Orange or any other color which matches the color of the yarn. Wing: One strand of Glo Bug yarn tied in at the head of the fly. A wide variety of colors works well including chartreuse, steelhead orange and Oregon cheese.

There are two criteria for a good Great Lakes fly. The first is that it is easy to tie, and there is not another fly that is easier to tie than this one. Second is that it be effective. This fly has proven to be especially effective on spawning fish. Although this is really a rediscovery of the yarn fly, this particular pattern was originated by Hank Kawalerski.

KRYSTAL BULLET

Hook: Sizes 2 to 8. Thread: To match color of body. Tail: Krystal Flash. Body: Chenille—medium for larger flies and small for smaller sizes. Wing: Krystal Flash tied in around the hook near the eye. The thread is then wrapped to the eye. The tips should be facing forward when tied in. The Kystal Flash is then tied back by wraps approximately 1/8 to 1/4 of an inch behind the eye of the hook.

This pattern has worked well to entice some otherwise difficult fish into striking. It has worked especially well on chinook salmon.

MARK'S CARPET FLY

Hook: Egg style sizes 2 to 8. Thread: Orange. Body: 6 to 8, 2 inch or shorter strands of regular sewing yarn. Each strand is a different color ranging from white to bright red and everything in between. Tying instructions are the same as those for the Glo Bug.

The fly was originated by Mark Stothard and has proven to be very successful on holding and feeding fish on Lake Ontario tributaries. One or two strands of a bright color against other drab colors seems to be the best combination. Its success may be due to this contrast or that it represents a cluster of eggs.

NUCLEAR ROE BUG

Hook: Sizes 4 to 10. Thread: To match color of body. Body: Glo Bug yarn wrapped or dubbed onto the hook. A variety of body colors can be used. Wing: White Glo Bug yarn tied in around the hook so that it envelopes the body. The length of the wing should be slightly longer than the body.

The enveloped body seems to project a very realistic image of an egg. It has proven to be a very effective fly for steelhead and brown trout.

SALMON FLEA

Hook: Mustad 3906B or Tiemco 3769 sizes 8 to 12. Thread: To match body color. Tail: White Glo Bug yarn cut so that it extends approximately 1/8 to 1/4 of an inch past the body. The same should be tied in at the head. Body: Small chenille in colors of chartreuse, orange or red.

This fly has proven to be a very good egg imitation and attractor in clear water conditions. It works well on finicky, selective or sluggish steelhead or brown trout. Due to its low profile, it sinks easily, which also contributes to its effectiveness.

SCRAMBLED EGGS

Hook: Mustad 3906B or Tiemco 3769 sizes 4 to 10. Thread: To match color of fly. Body: Glo Bug yarn. Tie in a full width of Glo Bug yarn on top of the hook, at the head of the fly. Hold the bobbin approximately one inch over the hook so that the thread is positioned tightly, straight above the hook shank. While keeping the thread tight, grasp the yarn between the thumb and forefinger of the other hand, approximately one-half inch from where it is tied down. Push the yarn toward the hook eye so that the tight thread splits the loose yarn in the middle. Wrap the thread away and at a slight angle toward the hook bend, tying down one-half of the loose yarn. This forms the first egg. Make the same wrap one more time. Then wrap the thread so that it ties down the other half of the loose yarn to form the second egg. Repeat the process three more times. Clip the yarn at the hook bend. Wrap the thread back to the hook eye by retracing the original wraps, form the head and tie it off.

The size of the eggs can be controlled by the amount of loose yarn pushed past the tight thread. This pattern creates the look of an egg cluster and with some practice, can be a very good looking imitation. A wide variety of colors are effective.

This pattern was originated by New York angler John Miller. It is very effective on holding and feeding fish. The fly almost has the appearance of a bait fisherman's egg sac. For this reason, an angler who is switching to fly fishing from bait fishing may find instant confidence in this pattern.

SMEGG

Hook: Egg style sizes 2 to 8. Thread: To match color of body. Tail: Two colors of Glo Bug yarn with one color being longer and surrounding the other. Also a few strands of Krystal Flash. Body: Various colors of chenille.

This pattern was originated by Salmon River guide and lodge manager Kent Appleby. It is a good pattern for steelhead. It can be tied in a wide variety of color combinations.

SPARKLE EGG

Hook: Mustad 3906B or Tiemco 3769 sizes 4 to 10. Thread: Orange. Body: Red or orange Spectra Chenille or Estaz tied in at the butt of the hook and wrapped forward to the eye. Actually a variety of colors work well. Pearl and purple have also proven to be effective.

This is a simple fly which has a translucent and enticing appearance in the water.

STARBURST

Hook: Mustad 3906B or Tiemco 3769 sizes 4 to 10. Thread: To match color of fly. Body: Rear 2/3 fine strand of wool yarn, front 1/3 Estaz.

This is a good pattern to use on holding fish as well as spawners. This pattern can be tied in a wide variety of colors. Those tied with chartreuse and cherise wool have proven to be very effective.

TWO BALL TOM CAT

Hook: Sizes 0/1 to 8. Thread: Orange. Body: Two separate Glo Bugs tied in the same manner as described earlier. The small space between the Glo Bugs is covered with thread. The pattern seems most effective when the Glo Bugs are different colors. Combinations of chartreuse, cherise, light roe, steelhead orange and flame seem to work best. Wing: White maribou.

This pattern was originated by Mike Keller and is an advancement of Dave Whitlock's two egg sperm fly. Tied in large sizes, this pattern has proven to be very effective on chinooks in the tributaries.

NATURAL PATTERNS

BUZZHEAD

Hook: Sizes 4 to 8. Thread: Black. Tail: Black squirrel tail. The cut ends of the squirrel tail pointing toward the hook eye should not be cut again as they are to be used for the wing case. Abdomen: Black chenille approximately 2/3's of the way up the hook shank. Thorax: Black chenille wrapped in thicker than the abdomen. Hackle: Black wrapped through the thorax. Wing case: Ends of the same black squirrel tail used for tail.

This fly was originated by Michigan guide Mike Gnatkowski along with his fishing companions. It is a simple but effective stonefly pattern. It can also be tied with variegated chenille of light and dark brown to represent the Hexagenia nymph. Red fox squirrel tail is used for the tail and wing case in this variation.

CADDIS LARVAE

Hook: Mustad 3906B or Tiemco 3769 sizes 6 to 12. Thread: Black or brown. Body: Dubbed fur. Bright green, olive or brown are the most common colors for the body. Head: Peacock herl or dark brown dubbing.

A good pattern to use on fall and winter holding fish. It is especially effective in tributaries of rich water quality where good numbers of caddis are naturally found.

CRAYFISH

Hook: Sizes 2/0 to 8. Thread: Black or olive. Tail: Fox squirrel tail or bucktail approximately the length of the hook shank split to represent the pinchers. Body: Olive chenille. Legs: Four strands of pheasant tail tied into the body on each side. Ribbing: Light copper wire. Overbody: Brown

Egg and natural patterns are a good choice for feeding or holding steelhead. Jerry Kustich displays a fresh steelhead which fell for a Glo Bug.

EGG PATTERNS

GLO BUG **MARK'S CARPET FLY** **SMEGG**

GLO BOU **NUCLEAR ROE BUG** **SPARKLE EGG**

HANK'S SPECIAL **SALMON FLEA** **STARBURST**

KRYSTAL BULLET **SCRAMBLED EGGS** **TWO BALL TOM CAT**

NATURAL PATTERNS

BUZZHEAD

CADDIS LARVAE

CRAYFISH

DEER HAIR BUG

EGG SUCKING LEECH

GREAT LAKES STONEFLY

SPRING WIGGLER

TEENY NYMPH

WET FLIES

BETSIE SPECIAL

BLACK BEAR GREEN BUTT

CHARTREUSE POLAR

CREASY COMET

CRICK

DOCTOR TOM

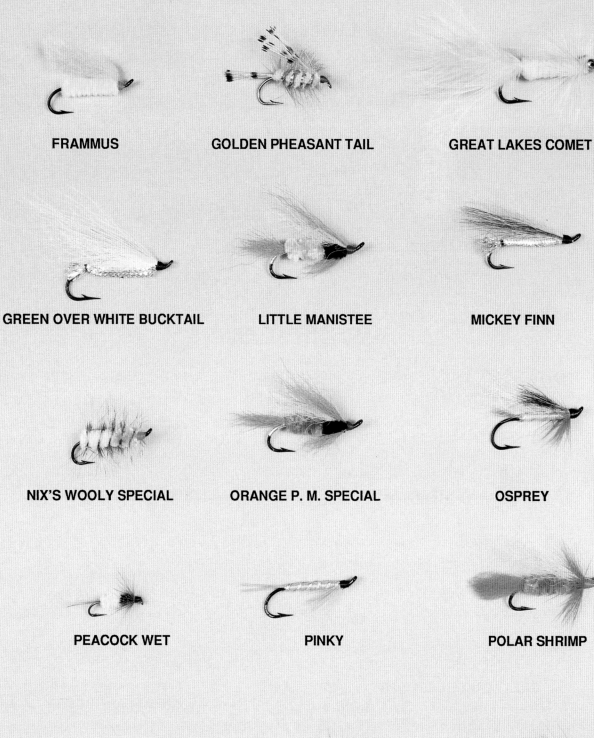

FRAMMUS   **GOLDEN PHEASANT TAIL**   **GREAT LAKES COMET**

GREEN OVER WHITE BUCKTAIL   **LITTLE MANISTEE**   **MICKEY FINN**

NIX'S WOOLY SPECIAL   **ORANGE P. M. SPECIAL**   **OSPREY**

PEACOCK WET   **PINKY**   **POLAR SHRIMP**

PSYCHO   **ROYAL COACHMAN**   **SALMON RIVER SUNSET**

SIMMY'S SPECIAL DARK

WINAN'S WIGGLER

WOOLY BUGGER

UGLY BUGGER

ZINGER

BAITFISH PATTERNS

BUNNY STREAMER

CLOUSER'S DEEP MINNOW

GREAT LAKES DECEIVER

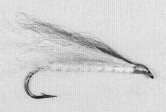

**LITTLE RAINBOW TROUT-
GREAT LAKE STYLE**

RAP FLY

WHITE ZONKER

turkey feather tied in at the tail and tied down at the eye with a portion allowed to protrude past the hook eye to represent the flipper. Lighter feathers can be colored with a waterproof marker.

Lead Eyes can be added to this pattern for fishing deep. They can also enhance the natural action of this fly. It is a simple pattern that has proven to be effective on everything from smallmouths to lake trout.

DEER HAIR BUG

Hook: Mustad 37189 or Tiemco 8089 sizes 2/0 to 4. Thread: Black or green. Tail: Six grizzly saddle hackles, three tied on each side to flare out. Hackle: Five or six wraps of grizzly hackle. Legs: Two or three rubber legs on each side. Head: Clipped deer hair.

This is basically a simplified version of Dave Whitlock's Deer Hair Bug. It can be tied in a variety of colors. Yellow/green is a popular combination to represent the natural colors of a frog. The head can also be clipped in the shape of a frog's head. This is a proven pattern on Great Lake's smallmouths, largemouths and even northern pike. Smaller sizes work well on some panfish. This fly is designed to be fished on the surface using the retrieve method. The Dahlberg Frog and the Whitlock Hair Water Pup are also good surface flies for warm water species in the tributaries.

EGG SUCKING LEECH

Hook: Sizes 2 to 6. Thread: Black or olive. Tail: Black or olive maribou. Body: Black or olive chenille for approximately 3/4 or more of the body. The body is completed by adding orange or red chenille in the shape of a ball.

This is an Alaskan pattern that represents a leech stealing an egg from a nest. This may never really happen on the Great Lakes tributaries but it sure is an effective pattern when fished around spawning beds.

GREAT LAKES STONEFLY

Hook: Mustad 3906B or Tiemco 3769 sizes 2 to 12. Thread: Black. Tail: Black hackle fibers or goose biots. Body: Black dubbing. Legs: Black hackle either wrapped through the thorax or tied in at the head. Wing pad: Black or brown turkey feather.

This simple pattern has a realistic appearance. Large sizes have worked well enticing fish on or near their beds. Smaller sizes (8 to 12) imitate the small black stonefly found on most Midwestern rivers. A wide variety of other effective stonefly patterns do exist.

SPRING WIGGLER

Hook: Sizes 4 to 12. Thread: Black or brown. Tail: Fox squirrel tail. Body: Cream yarn. Hackle: Brown palmered through the body. Overwing: Fox squirrel.

This pattern was originated by Ron Spring of Muskegon, Michigan. It is a very popular and effective pattern in the Midwestern Great Lakes area and is the main fly for many Great Lakes steelheaders.

TEENY NYMPH

Hook: Teeny nymph hook, Mustad 3906B or Tiemco 3769 sizes 6 to 12. Thread: Black. Body: Teeny Nymph pheasant tail wrapped to the head. Throat: Teeny Nymph pheasant tail tips.

This simple design was originated and patented by West Coast salmon and steelhead expert Jim Teeny. This pattern has worked magic on coastal rivers for years and has shown to be an effective pattern on Great Lakes salmonids as well. Best colors are black, lime green and purple.

WET FLIES

BETSIE SPECIAL

Hook: Sizes 2 to 10. Thread: Black. Tag: Silver Tinsel. Tail: Red calf tail. Butt: Silver Tinsel. Body: Rear 2/3 black chenille, front 1/3 red chenille. Throat: Black calf tail. Wing: Black calf tail.

This fly was originated by Michigan angler Dave Borgeson and named after Michigan's Betsie River. It was designed as a steelhead fly. In larger sizes it is a good high, off color water fly.

BLACK BEAR GREEN BUTT

Hook: 2/0 to 10. Thread: Black. Tail: Black calf hair. Butt: Chartreuse chenille. Body: Black chenille. Ribbing: Silver tinsel. Wing: Black calf hair.

In larger sizes this fly has proven to be one of the best for enticing a strike from a chinook on its spawning bed. The color combination seems to be the key to its success. The Green Butt Skunk is another traditional pattern which has proven to be very effective.

A selection of Great Lakes wet flies.

CHARTREUSE POLAR

Hook: Sizes 2/0 to 10. Thread: Chartreuse or yellow. Tail: Chartreuse hackle fibers or a thin strand of chartreuse Glo Bug yarn. Wing: White calf tail. Hackle: Chartreuse saddle tied in wet fly style.

This is my chartreuse version of the polar shrimp. Chartreuse is an effective color in the Great Lakes tributaries and this fly has proven deadly on lake-run salmonids.

CREASY COMET

Hook: Egg style sizes 2 to 8. Thread: To match color of fly. Tail: Axxel flash. Body: Chenille. Wing: Axxel flash.

This pattern was originated by New York and Pennsylvania guide Troy Creasy. Axxel flash is a new material that seems to have special fish enticing abilities. This pattern can be tied in a wide variety of color combinations. In the fall of 1991, using this pattern with blue Axxel flash and an orange chenille body, Troy guided one of his clients to a 47 pound 13 ounce chinook salmon which is now the New York State record. A chartreuse and purple combination of this pattern has proven to be very effective on big brown trout.

CRICK

Hook: Sizes 2 to 10. Thread: Black. Tail: Black calf tail. Butt: Fluorescent pink chenille. Body: Black chenille. Throat: Black calf tail. Underwing: White calf tail. Overwing: Black calf tail.

This fly was originated by Michigan angler and fly tier George Richey. It is a very good fly for dirty water conditions and for spooky fish.

DOCTOR TOM

Hook: Mustad 3906B or Tiemco 3769 sizes 2 to 10.

Thread: Orange or red. Body: Orange chenille. Hackle: Red and white palmered through the body. Overwing: Chartreuse Glo Bug yarn tied down at the head. The yarn should be clipped to within 1/4 to 1/2 of an inch of where it is tied down at the head.

This is a popular Midwestern steelhead pattern, originated by Tom Seroczynski and shown to me by Michigan guide Jim Rigby. A good variation of this pattern substitutes Spectra Chenille or Estaz for the palmered hackle. The overwing is clipped tight. A variety of body colors are used with this pattern from chartreuse to red.

FRAMMUS

Hook: Sizes 4 to 12. Thread: Orange or other to match color of fly. Body: Chenille. Wing: Thin strand of Glo Bug yarn extending just past the end of the body.

This fly was shown to me by New York guide Fran Verdoliva. It has proven to be one of the most effective patterns for steelhead, brown trout and even salmon. It is also extremely easy to tie. This pattern works well on holding fish as well as spawning ones. A variety of color combinations utilizing chartreuse, orange, red and white will catch fish. The best combination seems to be a chartreuse body with a steelhead orange Glo Bug yarn wing.

GOLDEN PHEASANT TAIL

Hook: Mustad 3906B or Tiemco 3769 sizes 4 to 12. Thread: Yellow or brown. Tail: Golden pheasant tail. Body: Yellow chenille. Ribbing: Gold tinsel. Wing: Golden pheasant tail. Hackle: Brown or grizzly palmered through the body.

This fly was originated by New York angler John Miller. It is a very effective pattern for fishing the brown trout run in the Lake Ontario tributaries.

GREAT LAKES COMET

Hook: 2/0 to 10. Thread: To match color of fly. Tail: Chartreuse maribou approximately the length of the body. Body: Chartreuse chenille. Hackle: Chartreuse saddle hackle. Eyes: Silver bead chain. Lead Eyes can be used for deep water flies.

Other colors such as black, orange and purple are also very good. The main difference between this tie and the West Coast style is the maribou tail. The action of maribou in the water really seems to entice fish into striking. This is an effective pattern for spawning fish. As a result of the weight of the eyes, it is an excellent fly for deep or heavy water.

GREEN OVER WHITE BUCKTAIL

Hook: 2/0 to 8. Thread: Black. Body: Silver mylar tubing. Underwing: White bucktail. Overwing: Chartreuse bucktail.

A white tail can also be added along with a few strands of flashabou in the wing. Blue is also a very good color for the overwing. This pattern is very effective on spawning fish, especially chinooks and coho salmon. In addition, this fly can be tied on 3x long or tandem hooks. Tied in this fashion they become very effective baitfish patterns for fishing the lakes.

LITTLE MANISTEE

Hook: Sizes 2 to 10. Thread: Red. Tag: Silver tinsel. Tail: Orange calf tail. Body: Rear 2/3 pink chenille, front 1/3 black chenille. Wing: 1/2 orange, 1/2 yellow calf tail with orange on top. Throat: Orange calf tail.

This pattern was created by Michigan angler David Borgeson and is named after Michigan's Little Manistee. It is an excellent steelhead fly under most conditions.

MICKEY FINN

Hook: Sizes 2 to 10. Thread: Black. Body: Flat silver tinsel with a silver oval tinsel rib. Wing: Equal amounts of yellow, red and yellow bucktail or calf tail tied in that order.

This traditional pattern is a very good attractor. It works well on salmon and steelhead when they are on or near their spawning beds.

NIX'S WOOLY SPECIAL

Hook: sizes 4 to 10. Thread: Orange or pink. Body: Rear half chartreuse chenille, front half pink chenille. Hackle: Grizzly palmered through the body.

Originated by New York guide Fran Verdoliva, it is a simple yet effective steelhead pattern.

ORANGE P. M. SPECIAL

Hook: Sizes 2 to 10. Thread: Orange or red. Tag: Silver tinsel. Tail: Orange calf tail. Butt: Silver tinsel. Body: Rear 2/3 orange chenille, front 1/3 black chenille. Throat: Orange calf tail. Underwing: Yellow calf tail. Overwing: Orange calf tail.

This pattern was originated by Michigan angler David Borgeson and named after Michigan's Pere Marquette River. The Red P. M. Special simply substitutes red chenille for the orange on the body. Both are excellent attractor patterns for steelhead and can also be used at times when fish are feeding on eggs.

OSPREY

Hook: Sizes 2 to 10. Thread: Black. Tail: Orange hackle fibers. Body: Chartreuse floss ribbed with silver oval tinsel. Underwing: Chartreuse calf tail. Overwing: Gray squirrel tail. Throat: Orange saddle hackle.

This pattern was originated by Mark Stothard. Chartreuse and orange along with the subtle overwing seem to provide an effective combination. It is a very good fly for spawning salmon and steelhead.

PEACOCK WET

Hook: Mustad 3906B or Tiemco 3769 sizes 6 to 10. Thread: Black. Tail: Brown hackle. Body: Rear half chartreuse chenille, front half peacock herl. Hackle: Brown hackle tied in wet fly style.

In small sizes this fly has proven to be a killer on lake-run brown trout and steelhead.

PINKY

Hook: Sizes 2 to 10. Thread: Black or pink. Tail: Pink hackle fibers. Body: Pink floss. Ribbing: Silver oval tinsel. Throat: Pink saddle hackle.

This pattern was originated by Mark Stothard. Its appearance is rather subtle yet is bright enough to act as an attractor. For this reason this pattern is a good choice as an attractor for spooky or cautious fish.

POLAR SHRIMP

Hook: Sizes 2 to 10. Thread: Orange. Tail: Red hackle fibers or flame Glo Bug yarn. Body: Orange chenille. Wing: White calf tail. Hackle: Orange saddle tied in wet fly style.

This traditional West coast pattern is very effective on the Great Lakes tributaries. Its natural colors allow it to be fished in a natural presentation as well as those techniques that allow the fly to swing in the current.

PSYCHO

Hook: Sizes 2 to 10. Tag: Sparkle 'n Stuff or Flashabou. Body: Fine strand of wool yarn. Rib-

bing: Fine silver tinsel. Wing: Axxel flash.

This pattern was originated by Salmon River guide and lodge manager Kent Appleby. Larger sizes work well on salmon and smaller sizes on steelhead. It can be tied in a wide range of color combinations. Red, chartreuse, blue, pink and purple are good choices for the body. Pearl and rainbow have proven to be effective for the Axxel flash wing.

ROYAL COACHMAN

Hook: Sizes 2 to 10. Thread: Black. Tail: Brown hackle fibers or red fox squirrel tail. Body: Peacock herl, red floss or yarn, peacock herl. Wing: White calf tail. Hackle: Brown, tied in wet fly style.

This traditional wet fly pattern has proven to work very well on spawning salmonids.

SALMON RIVER SUNSET

Hook: Sizes 2 to 10. Thread: Orange. Tail: Squirrel tail dyed red. Body: Purple floss. Hackle: Pink saddle hackle tied in wet fly style.

This pattern was originated by New York guide Fran Verdoliva. The color combination reminds him of the numerous sunsets he has witnessed while fishing the Salmon River area. Not only is it a pretty fly but an effective one as well.

SIMMY'S SPECIAL DARK

Hook: Sizes 2 to 10. Thread: Black. Tail: Red fox squirrel tail. Body: Olive chenille. Ribbing: Gold flat tinsel. Wing: Red fox squirrel tail. Throat: Red fox squirrel tail.

This pattern was originated by Simmy Nolph of Baldwin, Michigan. Its drab color scheme is very effective on spawning steelhead in clear water conditions.

WINAN'S WIGGLER

Hook: Sizes 2 to 10. Thread: Orange or red. Tail: Orange calf tail. Body: Yellow chenille. Hackle: Red saddle hackle. Overwing: Orange calf tail.

This pattern was originated by Michigan angler and fly tier George Richey and named after his fishing partner Larry Winan. Although patterned after the Spring Wiggler, this fly more closely imitates drifting spawn. For this reason it is an effective pattern on feeding as well as spawning fish.

WOOLY BUGGER

Hook: Sizes 2/0 to 10. Thread: To match color of fly. Tail: Maribou. Body: Chenille. Hackle: Saddle hackle palmered through the body.

This is an extremely effective pattern, especially for spawning fish. If the angler were limited to just two patterns to fish the tributaries, the Glo Bug and the wooly bugger would be the flies. The wooly bugger can be tied in a wide range of colors including black, olive, purple, chartreuse, yellow and orange. One of the best combinations is a black tail, olive body and black hackle. Lead Eyes can be added to the head for fishing deep or heavy water. Another variation of this pattern is to include a few strands of Flashabou in the tail.

UGLY BUGGER

Hook: 2/0 to 6. Thread: Black. Tail: White maribou. Body: White chenille. Hackle: White or cream saddle hackle palmered through the body. Wing: White maribou.

I took the wooly bugger another step further and created an extremely effective pattern for just about anything that swims in the Great Lakes. It seems to imitate a baitfish as well as being an attractor. With Lead Eyes, this is a top choice when fishing the hop method. Chartreuse is also an effective color.

ZINGER

Hook: 2 to 8. Thread: Orange or red. Tail: Red maribou. Body: Flame Glo Bug yarn, one strand tied in at a time and trimmed like the method used to tie a Glo Bug. The body should be trimmed evenly. The Glo Bug yarn can be tied in just on the top of the hook or on the bottom as well to form a fuller body. Wing: White maribou.

This is one of my own creations. This pattern has been extremely effective on steelhead, especially when it is combined with one of the methods that utilizes the swing of the current. The combination of bright colors and the movement of the maribou creates an irresistible combination. Best results have occurred with this pattern when the water is slightly off-color.

BAITFISH PATTERNS

BUNNY STREAMER

Hook: Mustad 3665A, Tiemco 300 or tandem style using Mustad 34007 sizes 2/0 to 4 tandem. Thread: Black. Tail: White maribou. Body: Pearl mylar tubing. Underwing: White rabbit strip. Overwing: Chartreuse or blue Krystal Flash.

This is a good pattern for fishing the lakes. It has accounted for many salmonids in the springtime. Due to its natural movement when in the water, it is an excellent choice when drifting or trolling.

CLOUSER'S DEEP MINNOW

Hook: Mustad 3906B or 9672, Tiemco 3769 or 5263 sizes 2 to 8. Thread: Black, or to match color of the fly. Eyes: Lead Eyes. Lower wing: White bucktail. Middle wing: Rainbow Krystal Flash. Upper wing: Pale gray or chartreuse bucktail.

This fly was developed as a smallmouth bass pattern by Pennsylvania guide, fly tier and

This steelhead was fooled by a simple wet fly.

shop owner Bob Clouser. Fly fishing expert Lefty Kreh commented in an article in *Fly Fisherman* that, "I don't know of a better underwater fly." At the time this seemed like quite a billing for such a simple design. However, in a short period of time, this pattern has taken just about every gamefish in the Great Lakes. It has worked well in the lakes on feeding fish and in the tributaries on spawners. There are other combinations in the Clouser's series. The two described have performed the best in the Great Lakes area.

GREAT LAKES DECEIVER

Hook: Mustad 9672 or 34007, Tiemco 5263 sizes 2/0 to 4. Thread: Black. Tail: Six chartreuse saddle hackles with three tied in on each side to flare out from the fly. A few strands of pearl flashabou should be added to the tail on each side. Body: Pearl mylar tubing. Wing: White bucktail tied in evenly around the shank of the hook. Chartreuse bucktail is then added to the top of the hook. Chartreuse Krystal Flash is then added on top of this.

This fly is basically a version of Lefty's Deceiver, which is a very effective saltwater fly developed by fly fishing expert Lefty Kreh. Since chartreuse is an effective color on the Great Lakes, this particular color combination has accounted for more than its fair share of Great Lakes trophies.

LITTLE RAINBOW TROUT - GREAT LAKES STYLE

Hook: Mustad 79580 or Tiemco 5263 sizes 2 to 8. Thread: Black. Tail: Chartreuse bucktail. Body: Cream or pink yarn or chenille. Ribbing: Silver oval tinsel. Wing: Layered wing of fine bucktail. First white or pink bucktail, then orange bucktail, then chartreuse bucktail and finally olive bucktail. A few strands of chartreuse Krystal Flash should be added between the chartreuse and olive bucktail.

This is a traditional bucktail pattern which has been modified to have a brighter appearance for use in the Great Lakes. Though it works well as a baitfish imitation, it is one of the most effective patterns for enticing spawning steelhead. Since it is such a big and bright pattern, it is a good one to use in muddy water conditions.

RAP FLY

Hook: Mustad 3665A, Tiemco 300 or tandem style using Mustad 34007 sizes 2/0 to 2 tandem. Thread: Black. Body: Silver mylar tubing. Wing: First layer—a long white maribou feather, second layer —healthy bunch of chartreuse bucktail or Fishhair, third layer—chartreuse or pearl Krystal Flash. Top layer—four chartreuse saddle hackles to form a baitfish silhouette.

Most flies are tied to represent a natural food source. This one is tied to represent an imitation. One particular spring a friend of mine did very well in Lake Ontario with a chartreuse jointed Rapala. I tied this pattern to represent the

Baitfish patterns work very well on lake trout.

basic color scheme of the Rapala. It has worked very well. It is normally tied big, almost 4 inches in length. Since it is a big pattern it can be difficult to cast. For this reason this pattern is best used while drifting or trolling in the boat when only short casts are normally required.

WHITE ZONKER

Hook: Mustad 9672 or 79580, Tiemco 5263 sizes 2 to 6. Thread: Red or black. Body: Pearl mylar tubing. Wing: White rabbit strip tied down near the bend of the hook and at the eye. The strip should extend past the bend of the hook by 1/2 to 1 times the length of the body. Throat (optional): Red maribou or hackle fibers.

This pattern has proven to be the best baitfish pattern for feeding lakers, browns and steelhead in the Great Lakes or in the tributaries. The undulating motion of the rabbit fur and the life-like portion of the strip which extends past the hook bend create a very life-like appearance, even when the fish gets a good look at the fly. Other color rabbit strips also work, such as black or chartreuse.

CHAPTER 8

Hooking and Landing Your Trophy

Landing fish the size of what an angler can expect to encounter in the Great Lakes takes proper equipment, skill and sometimes just plain luck. The action on or near the tributaries will not always be fast. As a matter of fact, there are many times when the angler may have to work hard to get a strike. So as not to waste opportunities that are the result of significant effort, the Great Lakes fly fisher should understand the elements of landing large fish in order to consistently bring them to the net. This chapter discusses what an angler can do to increase his or her odds.

SETTING THE HOOK

This seems like a pretty basic item, but any successful battle with a trophy fish begins with a good hook set. Quick and proper detection of a strike is usually the key ingredient. As discussed in chapter 5, the angler should be rigged up in a manner that facilitates proper detection. The lines used and the weight added to the leader should be enough to get the fly to the fish, but it should not be so much that it constantly hangs up on the bottom. If the fly hangs up on the bottom too often, the angler will become complacent, thinking that every time the fly stops, that it is simply being caused by the bottom. When a fish really does take, the angler may first think it is a hang-up and not give a proper set. The angler really needs to be in tune with the fly, and with focused concentration, must be able to confidently react to the take of a fish.

Most Great Lakes salmonids, especially large male chinooks and steelhead, possess very hard, boney mouths which provide for some low hook-up ratios and many lost fish. Some steps do exist that the angler can take to improve the chances. Razor sharp hook points are imperative. Chemically sharpened hooks that are sharp right out of the package seem to perform best. Unfortunately, a hook does not always stay sharp. Bottom obstructions take their toll on a hook point. The angler must continually check the hook point for any damage. Keeping hooks sharp with a honing file will result in greater success.

Another item which improves hook penetration is the use of hooks with small or no barbs. Some of the new hooks produced today are manufactured with smaller barbs. If using hooks where the barbs seem large, they should be crushed down slightly with forceps. Smaller barbs do not seem to increase the amount of lost fish like many might think. In other words, the advantages of better hook penetration seem to offset any possible disadvantages that using small barbs may have. In addition to this, small barbs allow for an easier, less harmful release of the fish.

In many of these fish with hard armored mouths, the only soft spot where the hook seems to bury deep is in the corner of the fish's mouth. For this reason, it is the preferred spot to put a hook point. There is a step the angler can take towards more frequent side-of-the-mouth hookups. By attempting to set the hook at a side angle, the fly will tend to sweep across the fish's mouth and the

The hard armored mouth of a male steelhead.

likelihood of a side-of-the-mouth hookup increases. Once the take has been detected, the hook set should be a hard, sharp movement. The strongest tippet that the angler can use for the conditions is helpful.

In situations where very light tippets must be used, the angler will need to control the hook set and replace strength with finesse. In situations where there is adequate tippet strength, the fly fisher should try to bury the hook as deep as it will go with a couple additional sets of the

hook. This should only be attempted when the fish is moving away. When the fish is at this angle, any pressure that is put on the hook should deepen the penetration. However, when the fish is sideways or facing toward the angler, additional sets of the hook may actually pull the hook out of its mouth.

LANDING THE FISH

After a successful hook set, the battle is on! Landing a trophy Great Lakes fish in a tributary, especially a steelhead or salmon, may take more skill than did the actual hooking. Fighting large fish can be very different from fighting and landing the small-to-medium size fish which are normally associated with the use of a fly rod. The angler should start out by getting any excess line onto the reel and by fighting the fish from the reel as opposed to simply stripping with the line hand. Fighting a fish from the reel provides for greater control and allows the angler to utilize the reel's drag system.

Many times the angler will need to take the fight to the fish in order to tire it out. In other words, constant pressure will have to be applied to keep the fish moving and fighting. This is especially true of a spawning fish which may have just one thing on its mind. Sometimes when a fish is

hooked which is intent on spawning, it will attempt to remain near the spawning bed. The angler may need to apply force to lead the fish away from this distraction so that it can focus on the fight. It is important for the angler to realize that a hooked fish that is simply sitting in the current is expending little energy. In such a situation, the angler may need to pressure the fish to fight.

Pressure can be applied in a couple of ways. The most effective, when the fish is close to the angler, seems to be side pressure. To adequately apply side pressure, the rod should be held low, down around the angler's waist. The rod tip should be dropped down so that the rod is used in a plane parallel to the water. This positioning accomplishes two things. First, it allows for more of the fly line to be in the water. The drag created

The angler applies side pressure to gain better control over the fish.

by the large diameter of the fly line, combined with the current flow of the tributary, assists in tiring the fish. Second, and more importantly, it makes it easier for the angler to turn the fish's head which allows for greater control. By using this method and by asserting the required amount of pressure, the angler can move the fish and force the fight. Additionally, by running the rod hand up the rod to the top of the handle and by tucking the butt of the rod up against his or her waist, the angler can use his or her whole body to apply pressure.

As a fish moves farther from the angler, the side pressure technique becomes less desirable. The reason for this is that as more line is in contact with the water, the drag continues to increase. Excessive tension caused by this drag can result in a broken leader or the fly pulling free. Before the tension gets to this point, the angler should raise the rod tip high and perpendicular to the water. This will lift most or all of the line off the water and allow the angler to apply pressure from the top. This angle will usually get most of the leader away from the bottom which assists in preventing abrasion. Although the angler will not be able to control the fish as well using top pressure, properly applied, it will help tire the fish.

Fighting a big fish can put considerable strain on the wrist and forearm of the arm in charge of the rod. To relieve some of this strain and to increase the amount of pressure applied to the fish, along with gaining a little more control of the rod during the fight, the angler can slide his line hand up the rod. Doing this provides for increased leverage and makes it easier to control the fish. Some caution should be used when doing this, however. As the line hand moves further up the rod, the leverage continues to increase. As the leverage increases, less of the rod is being used to absorb the fight of the fish, and consequently the possibility of breaking the rod on the fish also increases. When using this technique, place the line hand about 6 inches above the top of the rod handle. As the fish is pressured toward the angler,

the rod tip begins to move in a direction away from the water. At this point the line hand should be slid back down to the reel and line should be gathered as the rod tip is allowed to move back toward the fish.

The discussion to this point has centered around applying pressure. Doing so will usually be a part of almost every fight. However, this is not to imply that Great Lakes fish are poor fighters. On the contrary, many fights start out with feverish runs, wild head shaking and sometimes acrobatic displays. When a big fish really wants to make a run, most of the time there is not much the angler can do but let it happen. When this is the case, a proper drag setting on the angler's reel is essential. During a run the fish will pull against the drag which will help to tire it. Too tight of a drag may cause the tippet to break or the hook to pull out. To loose of a drag may cause the fish to run too far. This results in a loss of control over the fish. Such a loss of control can result in the fish becoming tangled in an underwater obstruction. It can also result in a break-off or in the fly being pulled out by the extra tension caused by too much fly line on or in the water. When the run is over and the fish is willing to give up line, the angler should take it. If the fish begins to rest in the current, one of the pressure techniques should be applied. It is my belief that the angler should keep as close to the fish as possible. Contrary to some opinions on the subject, it seems that following a fish when it runs upstream or down gives the angler greater control of the fish. For this reason, it is recommended to follow the fish where possible.

Sometimes it is impossible to follow a fish due to water that is too deep or fast. Other times the angler is faced with a situation where a fish is heading toward trouble, like a submerged log or heavy rapids. In these situations, it is best that the angler makes a stand. Experience has shown that the probability of landing a fish seems to be greater by keeping a fish out of such disastrous conditions by adding extra pressure.

Sliding the line hand up the rod provides extra leverage.

The angle from which the fish is played can be used to the fly fisher's advantage. This is especially true when the angler is attempting to keep a fish out of some particular water. This is best illustrated by an example. Imagine a situation where an angler is fighting a fish with a series of heavy rapids below. The angler should take a position so that he or she is between the fish and the water that the fish it is being kept from. In this example the angler should take a position slightly downstream from the fish. With the pressure coming from downstream, many times it will force the fish to move upstream, away from the rapids. If the dangerous water is upstream, then the converse is true.

A good rule when fighting a Great Lakes trophy seems to be to try to keep the fish off balance. Never let it rest. Vary the method, amount and angle of the pressure. When the fish is nearing the point of landing, positioning is again important. Experience has shown that the same positioning as used in the above example is a good way to finish off a fish. The positioning should be slightly downstream from the fish, and side pressure should be applied to lead it to the net or shore.

To this point, the discussions related to landing fish have assumed that the angler is using a tippet with sufficient strength to handle applied pressure. This will not always be the case. In some situations, the angler will be forced to use very light tippets. When fighting a fish on such light tippets the fight becomes more of game of give and take where the angler must attempt to take in line when possible, but let the fish go when it wants to move. Again, keeping the fish off balance seems to be the key. The angler should try to lead the fish into slower water, and keep it there if at all possible. As much pressure as can safely be applied should be used. If the fish makes its way

into heavier current and cannot be budged because of the light tippet, there is one off-beat trick that has worked on a few occasions. Try twanging the tightened fly line like a guitar string. For some unknown reason, this tends to make the fish move, and oddly enough, usually towards the angler.

Catch and release fishing is becoming quite popular in the Great Lakes region and is supported by most conservation-minded anglers. It is my opinion that the beautiful fish caught in the tributaries and the lakes should be allowed to fight another day. The strongest tippet size which can be used for each given situation allows the angler to land the fish quicker and return it while it still has some energy to spare. A big net is a handy tool to have at the end of a battle. Not only does a net allow for an easier landing, but can prevent damage to the fish which is a very important consideration when spawning fish are involved. If the

*A successful
battle comes
to an end.*

111

The angler tails a salmon caught during the fall spawning run.

angler does not have a net, it is usually not a problem. Most of the time a fish can be easily landed by beaching it in water which has a slow current flow and a gradual rise to the shore. Also, salmon can be "tailed" quite easily by leading its head downstream and grabbing it firmly with the line hand at the base of the tail.

Most of the items discussed in this section so far dealt with the situations created by landing fish in the tributaries. Landing fish in the lake is usually much less complicated. Pressure can be applied in the same way as discussed, but since there is no current and plenty of room to fight the fish, landing it is usually an easier task in the lake. The basic principle of letting the fish run when it wants to and taking in line when it allows is the main thing the angler should be concerned with when landing a trophy-sized fish in the lake.

CHAPTER 9

Where to Go

A multitude of tributaries feed the Great Lakes. Due to planting programs, wandering fish and natural reproduction, almost every tributary and the lake water near its mouth represent some opportunity for the fly fisher. Some of these tributaries provide better opportunities than others depending on water quality, water flow, adequate cover, good spawning areas and the amount of fish that have been stocked in the tributary or its capacity for reproduction. In addition, due to factors such as water depth and casting room, some tributaries are more suitable for fly fishing than others.

Since some of the Great Lakes tributaries do rank much higher than others in the quality of their fishing experience, they deserve special mention. The objective of this chapter is to list some of the tributaries that are consistent producers. They are presented by state or province in alphabetical order. The sections are further subdivided by the lake that the tributary feeds. Once the angler has selected the tributary or area to fish, there are a number of approaches for learning the access points and the best water to fish. The easiest is to locate a fly shop or sporting goods store near the area to be fished. Normally such a shop can provide a wealth of information. Fishing guide books can also be extremely useful. Such books may provide maps detailing access points and information on the expected runs and stocking information. It seems as though good local guide books exist for many of the areas in the Great Lakes region.

Another effective and efficient way to learn new water is to use a guide. There is a quality network of guides developing throughout the Great Lakes. Many either specialize in fly fishing trips or run such trips exclusively. An experienced guide will usually do more than just simply show the angler the best water. A good guide should provide an experience that will be long remembered, and would, therefore, be worth the investment.

When to fish a tributary is as important as where to fish. Timing an outing so that it is near the peak of a particular run can make an enormous difference.

Some of the more popular tributaries receive much fishing pressure, especially on the weekends. By fishing during the week, the angler can improve the chances of a successful outing and many times find some solitude. There are a few other approaches for the angler that prefers not fishing with a crowd. Cold, rain or snow will deter many anglers from taking to the stream. Normally, rainy conditions are very favorable for tributary fishing. Usually there is no shortage of this type of weather in the Great Lakes region during spring and fall. Fishing on pleasant winter days can also provide peace and quiet. Hooking a couple of steelhead on a quiet winter day can create a memorable experience. Additionally, selecting some of the less famous tributaries can assist the angler in getting away from the crowded fishing conditions.

ILLINOIS

The state of Illinois has a relatively small amount of shoreline bordering the southwestern part of Lake Michigan. There is no quality tributary water in this area. However, salmon and steelhead are planted in the harbors of Diversy, Jackson and Waukegan, and good opportunities exist in the Lake Michigan waters in and around these harbors.

INDIANA

Though Indiana occupies the smallest amount of Great Lakes shoreline, some good fishing does exist. Indiana borders Lake Michigan along its southeastern shoreline. Good opportunities can be found in the Little Calumet River, Trail Creek and Salt Creek. In addition to their regular runs of steelhead, these tributaries each boast a run of summer-run Skamania steelhead. The Skamania also provide good action along the Indiana shoreline of Lake Michigan.

MICHIGAN

The state of Michigan borders along four of five of the Great Lakes. It has more shoreline than any other state and is filled with beautiful clear running tributaries. It is a fly fisher's paradise. Not only does Michigan possess numerous tributaries, but some famous ones as well. The Pere Marquette, which flows into Lake Michigan, has become the mecca for the Great Lakes anglers in search of a quality fly fishing experience for big fish. Its miles of riffles, runs and pools, along with tremendous

Not only does Michigan's Pere Marquette River produce excellent action, but it is also a very scenic waterway.

areas of spawning gravel and consistent runs of fish attract many anglers each year. A good portion of the runs are supported only by natural reproduction. The best fly fishing can be found downstream from Baldwin and includes a 7 mile "flies only" stretch from the M-37 bridge downstream to the Gleason's Landing access point.

A number of other tributaries of Lake Michigan possess similar characteristics to the Pere Marquette. Most have consistent runs, miles of fishable water and at least some natural reproduction. These tributaries normally run clear except for extreme rainfall or runoff. The list of other quality streams and rivers along the Lake Michigan shoreline includes the Betsie River, Grand River, Little Manistee River, Manistee River, Muskegon River, Pentwater River, Platte River, St. Joseph River and White River. The Pine River and Sturgeon River offer good opportunities along the Upper Peninsula portion of Lake Michigan. The lower end of some of these rivers consist of a bay before they dump into Lake Michigan. These bays are referred to as lakes themselves. Some good fly fishing for bass and walleye as well as lake trout can be found in these areas.

A number of the tributaries feeding Lakes Huron and Superior also provide good fly fishing opportunities. The following represent the best opportunity for a quality fly fishing experience: Lake Huron–Au Gres River, Au Sable River, Carp River, Ocqueoc River, Rifle River and Sturgeon River; Lake Superior–Chocolay River, Gratiot River, Middle Branch Ontoagon River, Sucker River and Two Hearted River.

MINNESOTA

The state of Minnesota possesses shoreline along the northwestern portion of Lake Superior. A characteristic common to many of the streams on the north shore of Lake Superior is that natural waterfalls often limit the area which can be fished for lake-run fish. Despite this some good fly

fishing exists. Almost any Minnesota stream or river feeding Lake Superior will have a run of fish up to its first barrier. Though some of these areas are short, others are not. The longest is the Knife River which has over 70 miles of fishable water. The Knife River has historically been Minnesota's best steelhead river. The water from Highway 61 to the lake, along with the upper and lower falls areas, provides the best opportunity for the fly fisher.

Good opportunities exist in other tributaries and the lake water near their mouths, even though most of the fishable portions of these tributaries consist of only a mile or less of water. These tributaries include the Baptism River, Brule (Arrowhead) River, Cascade River, Cross River, Lester River, Split Rock River, Stewart River and Sucker River. The Brule (Arrowhead) is the largest of these and has a mile and a half of fishable water and should not be confused with the legendary Bois Brule River in Wisconsin. The Sucker River has approximately 4 miles of water up to the first impassable barrier. The Baptism, Cascade and Lester Rivers receive heavy runs of chinook salmon. There are about 60 other fishable tributaries in the state of Minnesota.

NEW YORK

The state of New York borders both Lake Ontario and Lake Erie. In terms of fly fishing opportunity in the Great Lakes states, it probably ranks second only to Michigan. Lake Ontario is known for its large fish. Chinooks in excess of 40 pounds are taken each year, and the state record steelhead of 26 pounds and 14.8 ounces was also taken from Lake Ontario. The fish in Lake Erie and its tributaries normally average much smaller in size than in Lake Ontario. What is lost in size is more than compensated for by the picturesque nature of the Lake Erie shoreline and most of its tributaries.

New York is not lacking in famous spots to

fish either. The Salmon River which runs through Pulaski and flows into Lake Ontario may be the most well known of all Great Lakes tributaries. Unfortunately, this reputation has resulted in heavy fishing pressure at times. However, due to a better commitment towards sport fishing by some groups in the area, conditions continue to improve. The fly fisher can expect a quality experience on this river despite the amount of fishing pressure it receives because of its consistent runs. A small fly-fishing-only area was established during the 1990 season, and other such areas will hopefully be opened in the future.

The Niagara River, which is the link flowing from Lake Erie to Lake Ontario, is steadily building a reputation as a top quality tributary. The lower river which begins below Niagara Falls is probably the best big fish river in the Great Lakes, if not the entire lower 48 states. It is big water with opportunities existing for both boat and bank anglers. Trout and salmon can consistently be found in its waters from September to early June. Large smallmouths and walleyes can be found during the summer months.

New York's Salmon River may be the most popular of all Great Lakes tributaries. Its tremendous runs of fish are a main reason for this popularity.

A number of other tributaries exist along the Lake Ontario shoreline whose makeup and size is wide and varied. While some possess marginal water for this type of fishing, most represent a good opportunity for fly fishing. Some of the best fly fishing opportunities on Lake Ontario tributaries can be found on the Black River, Genesee River, Irondequoit Creek, Johnson Creek, Little Salmon River, Oak Orchard Creek, Oswego River, Perch River and South Sandy Creek.

Some good tributaries are also located along the Lake Erie shoreline. The best are Canadaway Creek, Cattaraugus Creek, Chautauqua Creek and Eighteen Mile Creek. Especially good opportunities exist at the mouths of each of these creeks. In addition, Lake Erie is host to some of the best trophy smallmouth bass fishing in North America. Smallmouths can be readily caught using the drift and retrieve techniques described in chapters 5 and 6.

OHIO

Ohio borders Lake Erie on its southwestern shore. Very good lake-run fishing, especially for steelhead, can be found in some of the Ohio tributaries. One such tributary which is steadily gaining popularity is the Rocky River, due to its consistent steelhead runs and its proximity to so many anglers. This river actually runs through the city limits of Cleveland.

Other quality tributaries in Ohio include the Chagrin River, Conneaut Creek, Grand River and Vermilion River. Conneaut Creek may be the most consistent of the Ohio tributaries while the Grand River probably draws the largest number of fish.

There is one item to be mindful of when it comes to southern Lake Erie tributaries. Clay banks border some of these bodies of water. The result is that such streams and rivers can dirty quickly after a heavy rain or runoff. Bright orange and hot red work well in Lake Erie streams when such off color conditions exist.

Good opportunities also exist for the fly caster along the shoreline of Lake Erie for steelhead, smallmouth bass and walleye.

ONTARIO

Like the state of Michigan, the Canadian province of Ontario also has shoreline along four of the Great Lakes. They are Lake Erie, Lake Huron, Lake Ontario and Lake Superior. Ontario is host to some excellent opportunities for quality Great Lakes fly fishing.

Along the north shore of Lake Superior there is nearly a countless number of tributaries. The beauty of this area is breathtaking. Almost all these tributaries have a good run of fish. The steelhead run in the streams and rivers in this area occurs later than in most other locations. The peak of the run is normally in May but can occur as late as early June. Lake trout can sometimes be found in the lower ends of some of these tributaries. This area also represents one of the best opportunities to catch a Great Lakes brook trout.

The remote nature of much of this northern shore area makes it easy for the angler to find peace and quiet. Actually, some of the tributaries require quite a hike. Here the angler can even find a true wilderness experience. Some of the fishable areas below the first impassable barrier are rather short. When fishing one of these tributaries for the first time the angler should make sure that he or she is fishing below this barrier. Some of the better tributaries feeding Lake Superior are the Agawa River, Baldhead River, Coldwater River, Michipicoten River, Montreal River, Old Woman River, and University River.

There is also some fine fly fishing in the tributaries along Lake Huron. The Saugeen River has gained the reputation as being one of the best Great Lakes tributaries. It is a picturesque river with good runs of salmon and some very large steelhead. Some of the other top quality tributaries located along Lake Huron are the Bighead River, Nottawasaga River and Sauble River.

The fly fishing opportunities in Ontario along Lake Erie and Lake Ontario are fairly limited. The best opportunities can be found along Lake Erie in Big Creek and Big Otter Creek, and along Lake Ontario in Bronte Creek, Credit River and Wilmot Creek.

PENNSYLVANIA

The state of Pennsylvania possesses a small stretch of the Lake Erie shoreline. Included in this area are some creeks which provide some fine steelhead and salmon action. Walnut Creek, located near the city of Erie, is one of the most popular and consistent producers. Elk Creek is the largest of the Pennsylvania tributaries. It receives excellent runs of fish and contains some of the best water for fly fishing.

Other good Pennsylvania tributaries include Crooked Creek, Racoon Creek, Sixteen Mile Creek, Twelve Mile Creek and Twenty Mile Creek. Some of the best action can sometimes be found near or at the mouth of the creek.

WISCONSIN

Wisconsin borders Lake Michigan along its western shoreline and Lake Superior on the south side of its western tip. The pride of this state's lake-run fishery is the Bois Brule or Brule River. This long, scenic river is a combination of pools, runs and gravel with a consistent run of fish and naturally reproducing steelhead. This combination of good fly fishing opportunity and truly beautiful surroundings creates the environment for a quality experience. Two other small tributaries which feed Lake Superior are the Cranberry River and Fish Creek.

On the Lake Michigan side there are a number of tributaries which have very good runs of fish and excellent fly fishing. The Kewaunee River has become one of the most popular tributaries along Wisconsin's Lake Michigan shoreline. It has water that is well suited for fly fishing and receives excellent runs of steelhead. The Manitowoc is another quality river. This is big water, but when it is running at the proper level, it can provide an excellent fly fishing opportunity.

Other tributaries located along the Lake Michigan shoreline are the Root River, Sheboygan River, Pigeon River, Branch River, East and West Twin Rivers, Onconto River, Peshtigo River and Menominee River. Sand Bay Creek and Stony Creek, although small in size, may represent the best chance for landing a Great Lakes brook trout. Three other small creeks located in Door County, Hibbards, Whitefish and Heins can be fishable when other rivers are running high.

Final Thoughts

Like almost all other great fisheries in North America, the Great Lakes and its tributaries face their share of problems. Snagging and other unethical conduct, overcrowded conditions, increased pressure on fish populations in the lakes by charter boat captains not practicing catch and release, disease, exotic species and pollution are the main problems threatening the quality of the Great Lakes fly fishing experience. There are some measures that the angler can take to improve or protect this fishery. Becoming involved in some of the groups dedicated to the protection of the resource may be the most important. On an individual basis, keeping abreast with current issues and supporting your views through letters to the proper congressmen and representatives can be very important. Such letters can significantly impact decisions concerning new laws and budget appropriations for programs designed to benefit the Great Lakes.

One of the biggest problems on the tributaries which receive high pressure is a lack of etiquette. It seems to stem from a general lack of knowledge as to the proper behavior on the stream or river, which in turn is normally due to inexperience and a lack of education. The education issue is something that is beginning to be dealt with by some states and local groups. If each angler took it upon himself to practice good stream etiquette, times of high fishing pressure could be tolerated much easier. The basic rule for good etiquette is to give the next angler as much room to fish as you would like him or her to give you. If each angler followed this simple principle and attempted to educate other anglers where possible, the fishing environment on some of our more crowded rivers would be greatly improved.

Bibliography

Brooks, Joe, *Trout Fishing;* Harper & Row, New York, 1972.

Elman, Robert, *The Fisherman's Field Guide to the Freshwater and Saltwater Gamefish of North America*; The Ridge Press, New York, 1977.

Ferguson, Bruce, and Johnson, Les, and Trotter, Pat, *Fly Fishing for Pacific Salmon*; Frank Amato Publications, Portland, 1985.

Fly Fisherman; Published by Cowles Magazines, Inc., Harrisburg, PA: vols. 16-22, 1985-1991.

Leiser, Eric, *The Complete Book of Fly Tying*; Alfred A. Knopf, Inc., New York, 1977.

McClane, A. J., *New Standard Fishing Encyclopedia*; Holt, Rinehart, and Winston, Inc., New York, 1974.

Migel, J. Michael, and Wright, Leonard M., Jr., editors, *The Masters on the Nymph*; Nick Lyons Books, New York, 1979.

Richey, David, *Great Lakes Steelhead Flies*; Sportman's Outdoor Enterprises, Inc., Grawn, MI, 1979.

Trout; Published by Trout Unlimited, Vienna, VA: vol. 30, no. 4.

Wedge, Les, *Lake Ontario Trout and Salmon Fishing*; New York State Department of Environmental Conservation, 1987.